THR

William Henry Searle, PhD, is a poet and writer whose work draws on personal lived experience, seeking to interweave the natural world with the human. He holds a doctorate in creative writing and environmental philosophy, for which he was awarded a three-year studentship at the Royal Holloway University of London. His first book, *Lungs of my Earth*, was published in the USA in 2015 by Hiraeth Press. He divides his time between Snowdonia and the New Forest, exploring, writing and wood carving.

THREADS

William Henry Searle

arrow books

10 9 8 7 6 5 4 3 2 1

Arrow Books
20 Vauxhall Bridge Road
London SW1V 2SA

Arrow Books is part of the Penguin Random House group of companies whose
addresses can be found at global.penguinrandomhouse.com.

Penguin
Random House
UK

First published in hardback by Century in 2019
First published in paperback by Arrow Books in 2020

www.penguin.co.uk

A CIP catalogue record for this book is available from the British Library.

Some of the pieces in *Threads* have previously been published
(in different form) as follows:

'The Ravens of Clogwyn Mawr', *Earthlines,* Issue 15, July 2016; 'The Lungs', 'The
Cormorant', 'The Stag', 'The Ewe' and 'The Seal', *Earthlines,* Issue 12, July 2015;
'The Hollow of Shell Bay', *Bellevue Literary Review*, May 2016; 'The Beech Tree',
Resurgence and Ecologist, January 2016; 'Living in the Shadow of the Rain', finalist in
the 2016 Barry Lopez Award for Non-fiction; '3,000 metres' (in 'Father'), *Voices of
the Wild: An Anthology of Nature Writing*, June 2016; 'Young Rain', *Equinox*, August
2012; 'The Stone Wall' and 'The Mute Swan', *Agenda*, Spring 2012; 'A Nocturnal
Pact', *The Salt Book of Younger Poets*, August 2011; 'Another Astronomy', *Days of
Roses II*, July 2013.

The publisher and author wish to thank Serpent's Tail for permission to quote from
The House of Breath by William Goyen.

ISBN 9781787462397

Printed and bound in Great Britain by Clays Ltd, Elcograf S.p.A.

Penguin Random House is committed to a sustainable future for
our business, our readers and our planet. This book is made
from Forest Stewardship Council® certified paper.

Gather the broken pieces, connect them: these are the only things we have to work with. For we have been given a broken world to live in – make like a map a world where all things are linked together and murmur through each other like a line of whispering people, like a chain of whispers a full clear statement, a singing, a round, strong, clear song of total meaning, a language within language, responding each to each forever in the memory of each man.

William Goyen, *The House of Breath*

For Elowen,
our baby girl, born sleeping
27.07.17.
Even though you are not with us,
you are our everything.

Contents

THREADS

Introduction

The curling of my wife's salt-flecked hair in the south-west wind, the glimmer of relief in her eyes. A lone bald eagle stretching out its wings, gesturing to gather in the whole sky, feather by feather. A dear friend's quiet company in a rolling white and silver sea of moonlit fern. In the pages to come are the beckoning particulars of life that make up networks of quiet wonder and awe. I have tried to capture these chance noticings, the common occurrences that widen the heart. The way the world of living things can hold our attention, draw us in, entwine us.

This book is not simply a book about the natural world, but about something wider and deeper: everyday, earthly life and our place within it – the discovery of kinship. For me, kinship is not a romantic notion preserved only in some golden age of wisdom; it is a concrete possibility even amidst the frenetic tide of everyday life. The only way back into the earth, into our animal senses, is by coming in close, paying attention to what has never left: our fundamental reliance on our natural surroundings. The division between what is nature and what is not nature can be dissolved, or at least made more permeable. This sense of kinship can become common, significant and necessary.

But finding this attitude can be a challenge. For example, our over-reliance on virtual technologies so often screens us from the real depths of experience, screens us from one another, blocks intimacy with other living, breathing beings. We must remember that we ourselves are bodies, flesh and blood. Technology can be a means of escape and communication perhaps, but we risk losing touch with what is natural to us: our primordial entanglement in the earth. Excessive interaction with the virtual breaks us away from what we, as bodies, yearn for: embracing what is close to us, intimacy with the people and places that surround us day after day. The commonplace is sometimes the most extraordinary place we could ever be.

Today presents us with a rich opportunity *to relate*. Even amidst the horrors of life, there is a chance to bridge the divide between ourselves, one another, and the natural world through intimacy, paying attention to the mysteries rather than agonising over their solutions, to start the long walk back home. We can so easily become distracted – lost in our virtual worlds, caught up in our work or family or pastimes, consumed by ever-evolving goals – while the critical work of intimacy remains in our blind spot and our attitude hardens into one of bland, expressionless indifference. I am not rejecting the pursuit of comfort through hard-earned money, nor am I rejecting the technologies that we, as a species, have assembled to improve our lives, nor the complexities of religion or politics that govern our beliefs and attitudes. These are all part of what it means to be human. But there is something vitally amiss in our daily lives. Which is: simply loving, amidst all our other pursuits, the sensuous world. The time and effort it takes to unobtrusively open yourself up to a person or place and, in turn, for that person or place to open up to you can be an enigmatic and uncertain process, one at odds with a cultural mainstream fixated on quick-fix material gains and instantaneous rewards. But it is within our capacity.

Trying to make sense of our chaotic presence on this earth can sometimes push us to the brink of despair. But if you allow it, through attention and patience, bare life will make sense of you. The need to make sense of *it* dwindles. The earth will carry on turning, the clouds will cast their scudding shadows, and the stars will shine upon the charred landscapes of the future. Stay with living things – the trees, the sky, the rain, the rocks, the very ground beneath your feet that supports not only you but those you love and those who love you in turn – and, in time, you'll be rocked into a rooted place, settled.

This book is made up of stories and poems – tender interrogations of episodes spent in close physical proximity to adored people and places – structured into seasons: from my obsession with ravens in the hills of Eryri (Snowdonia) to a day with my wife, Amy, spent in loving reverie clear of the bipolar II that has dogged her; from climbing mountains with my father, to hours spent in admiration of a beech tree, to feeling the kicks of our daughter Elowen as nightjars whirred away their arias to the night, never knowing that it would be one of the last times I felt her before she was born sleeping at full term. Woven into the four seasons – the great intertwined cycles of continuity and renewal – are quiet celebrations, a map of cherished connections, of which the above examples are a vital few. Beginning with my own infancy and continuing right through to our daughter Elowen, with family, extended family, animals, weather and places purled throughout, the book forms a kind of memoir that opens out towards the future, in which memory is not just what remains but what lends depth of experience to an appreciation of the present. All the pieces are fragments of a larger whole that is always taking shape through time, time that is not necessarily linear but rather a part of the wanings and waxings, the goings and comings that give life a certain and yet hard-to-pin-down rhythm, the seasons of existence.

Something else emerges out of the many embraces: a sense that these lives are *sacred*. As a word usually associated with religion, it is often considered arcane, separate from our daily conversations and contact with the world around us, reserved for the few who devote themselves to the holy – specialist and exclusive. But I do not believe that this is the whole story. I would say that our loved ones are sacred; the things of this earth are sacred too, even before we put the stamp of religion on them. This much more primal, mundane, bodily, earthly, accessible, and inclusive sense of the sacred comes about as a natural consequence of unobtrusively attending to things and caring for them, being a part of them, not wanting to possess them. Are not our loved ones sacred? Are not the lives of this earth sacred?

A sense of the sacred is created by beginning with what you know, who you know, where you know. That tree over there, this person, this river, that swathe of sky above home. Start small. The sacred is there before our very eyes. It is not an object to be bagged but a process to be lived through. We can breathe it and live it if we just wake up. The sacred is about rediscovery and allowing ourselves to be gently gathered into the earthly moment, and to stay there a while. It is a quality that is as earthly as the texture of bark, the sound of a wave. There is no need to calculate or control; the feeling of awe is the gift of mere sentience. Simply being present in a living, breathing, singing world, in that place of shimmering contact, is enough for life to flourish, for things to simply be themselves.

In such a way, the threads of life are pulled tight and plucked, relationships like chords resounding in the right key. Once in a while, be present. Be close. Be intimate. Stop, look, listen. Then get closer, nearer. Repeat the ritual. Allow yourself to turn aside from life's busy path, and appreciate what surrounds you. Rebel against the propensity to be a fugitive from the living world. There are other directions to travel than the ones we are thrown into. Make yourself available to things; surrender, revere. Deviate, once in a while, to breathe in life rather than blow it away.

Spring

Innocence

From a case in the attic she found rainbow laces
to tie round her ankles and wrists.
Now nobody, not even family and pets, can find
– though they see her – where she begins.

The Prism of Home

Mother. I celebrate her as the teacher of intimacy, the expert of love. She was the first person who held me, the one who defined my relationships with all subsequent others, places and people; my own range of intimacy with things dependent upon my openness to the intimacy that my mother practised and preached. It was within her that I grew and was nourished until I was born, till I breathed, screamed and searched for her to hold, demanding to be held, nourished once again. The first person. The beginning. The home of all homes. The primal witness of my becoming, the truest other through which my own being was woven. The origin to whom I owe my being. The unconditional gift of her to myself, the myself before 'the self', the blessed continuum, the necessary enclosure of myself within her before I was vaulted into the broken world, the separation crystallised, the leaving of that love.

She was the first landscape of protection, like the summer oak at the far end of the field that shelters me from a freak downpour of rain. The mountain cave, the damp and close darkness from which I peer out at lightning dancing across the storm-wracked plateau, clouds lowering with passive immensity, freighted with threatening shadow. The quiet space beneath the turning and rolling wave that would have hurled me shoreward onto the cold stones and the rocks, that carries me to a pool of undulating light. She was all those experiences of a kind of wild comfort, the way in and the way out of the world.

I must love my mother deeply, I must. I must remember her and live with her within me and walk with her, my being must be an expression of gratitude to her unflinching care. I must approach and gaze at and hold the things of this world with the loving intimacy that my mother taught me. I belong because she *is*. Hers is the face, the hands, the eyes, the voice of refuge. The body and symbol of all that can be good in us. The mother I love in the language of love that she speaks. My thanks to her are measured in the intimacy that I give to others; she is the giver of my very capability to relate. The care that comes from her pierces every object and refracts, spreads out into the world, riveted with the many colours of her love. The world can be a beautiful place if we dare to carry on that love within our doings, to live as though her love were imbued in our actions.

The first memories are of her love, the simple power of her presence, the way the surrounding world moved to her touch. Her gentle orchestrations of space into nearness and of time into something that does not run out but spreads and deepens, like a rising pool that lifts and supports me. She was my world in those earliest years I can remember and in the years that I cannot remember in mind but can in body.

The way she washed and cleansed me, the ceremony of that task before bedtime. She bathed me in peaceful water, pausing like a soloist mid-song to change rhythm, scooping, pouring with a Mauritian shell of roseate gloss and pearl patina, untying bags of steam, letting loose moths of lavender foam. White drizzle released down the silken slides of her wrists. Tempted to take a sip, I tasted its bitterness unlathering on my bottom lip. I was often shocked breathless by the cold ceramic touch of wet white tiles when I sleepily leaned too far, tipping the water's smooth balance. After picking out garden dirt from under my nails, scrubbing my heels smooth with a worn nub of pewter pumice, she prised open the chainless plug, adding to the tally of scratches on its big silver button, towel-dried each hair in diminishing mist, then left me clean to go bring new nightclothes, appearing with them in her cradling arms as though they were precious.

Night terrors wracked my early years. I would close my eyes and my eyes hardened and sank back deeply into my head. A pressure exerted itself into my brain. It felt as though my room was caving into me, the weight of the dark walls, the tile roof, the night sky itself, all collapsing not onto me but into me and through me, pinning me down onto the bed that hardened into something like concrete. Then, in a jolt, the world would fling out of me, hurling itself in countless wires and threads trailing off into an infinite distance, immense and yet small. The dream woke me with violent sickness and, though I was awake, the image and sensation of the world frayed into a million and one dark lines that lingered and burned into my body and mind. I was terrified and ran across the hallway into Mum and Dad's room, sneaking round the half-open door, peering at Mum as she lay upon the right side, as small as a child against Dad and in the largeness of the bed. I would creep up to her, holding myself, tearful but trying to be quiet, and loom over her, hoping to wake her without intrusion. Unflustered, she would extend her arm and fold it around me to bring me in close as though into the nook of a nest, and I lay beside her, safe from the nightmare, warm and full of sleep.

When Ollie passed – our eighteen-year-old Border terrier, limping and gristle-lump ridden to his last hours, my best friend, a brother – Mum and I took a trip out to the Isle of Wight, taking the ferry across the calm waters of the Solent on a clear and warm autumn day. Up on Tennyson Down, on the far western tip of the island, the sea glistening all around us, clouds flying south-west over us in an exhilarating wind, we spelled out Ollie's name in white chalk stone upon the green ground. It was our remembrance, our farewell. We scattered his ashes over the cliff edge, into the wind, and watched them disperse to invisibility, absorbed by the sea air he loved to sniff. I had a vision of him running back to us, up the sloping down, through the tall grasses, his stout body sinking left to right in happiness to greet us, his thick tail wagging, me and Mum calling his name, and just before he reached us vanishing like a smile, like the sun that autumn day, flaring out into darkness with the last beat of heart-coloured light, the chalk cliffs glowing watery crimson, Mum and I traipsing back along the downs to Freshwater Bay.

I am no longer dependent upon my mother. But she is still everything. The connection glistens still. I can look at her now the way she looks and looked at me, not in awe at her presence but as a human being shaped by time. The skin upon her hand, her eyes, the colour of her hair in the winter light as we take our walks across the heath or stand stock-still upon the sea wall, waiting for kingfishers, me pointing out the names of birds to her, exclaiming just as she once did to me. Love comes full circle but does not sterilise itself. It feeds itself in the charged circuit of its completeness like the passage of blood around the body, like the repeated refrains of the tides, like the movement of the seasons, the shape of the round earth. In her presence what ice may build up around my heart in an often hard and chill world thaws, melts, and runs, releasing the proper clamour of my warm heart, which beats in kinship with other beings, other things, other places.

The Lungs

Laid out on the central Formica table that almost spanned the width of Biology Room II, in a grey plastic tray was a pair of lungs. Sleek and creamy red, a display of flesh. Mr Stephens, the teacher, stood back from the organ, his arms folded across his chest. His black hair was swept over as far as it could reach to his right ear. The top button of his shirt was like a watchful eye in the inch gap between his collar and slackened tie. His hands locked in a grab beneath his armpits, pulling his shirt tight from around his back. A look of nervous expectancy was in his eyes as though he was waiting for his life-like sculpture to be scrutinised and judged. The lungs gleamed a moist red in the afternoon sunlight beaming in through the huge bay window that overlooked the fields and neighbouring woods and the undulating rooftops of the town beyond. Rooks paddled up from the canopies, stalled, then showered down and across the tops of the trees, flowing.

Added to the usual medicinal smell of the room was a cooler, earthy smell that strengthened as I neared the organ in mild horror and fascination, holding the tops of my bag straps, gawking forwards along with the rest of the class. Mr Stephens' expression relaxed into a half-smile of gentle smugness, his arms falling down to his sides as we confirmed his expectations with our various reactions to the frank display of the lungs. The girls shrieked and shuffled away in haste, a few boys merely peeked at the specimen with an air of heroic disregard and playful insensitivity, and some gazed at it with genuine curiosity until they were tugged back by the commands of Mr Stephens or shocked still by the butchery gore of the thing.

Snapping on a pair of white gloves, Mr Stephens strolled over to the lungs, gathering us close with a gesture of embrace. Bags tumbled off shoulders and fell to the linoleum floor in rustling thuds. Wriggling his fingers beneath the lungs, he slowly and carefully lifted them a foot above the tray, keeping his palms beneath each lung like a waiter presenting a terrine to hungry guests. Before he spoke, there was a moment of silence in which all eyes were open, all mouths agape. No one was exempt from the awe that the display of lungs imparted. The colours were astounding in the sunlight, the crimson sheen of the flesh seemed like lamination, plastic in its manicured brightness but lithe and supple in its yielding to Mr Stephens' rearrangement of his grip to the outer rims, holding them like wings, the central section sagging and widening to a gap below the jaundice-coloured trachea. They must have been heavy as his forearms swelled and shook under the pressure of holding them aloft, finding respite in lowering them into the tray, aware of their preciousness like a jeweller returning a spangling necklace to its velvet cushion.

Awe turned to respect – a certain boundary of distance grew between us and the object, felt as a dislocation – and then to knowing interest as Mr Stephens began to diligently present each part of the lungs, pointing, showing, naming. Trachea: firm like the hard fat prized from a rump steak. Left and right bronchi branching into bronchioles, clustered at the ends by alveoli. He went on, listing, describing the function of each part. He inserted a black rubber tube into the top of the trachea, and blew. The lungs distended, stretched out like oblong balloons, and then deflated as he removed his mouth from the tube. Air wheezed out from the chimney of the trachea, the details of the parts, the vivid purple lines, the crimson pleura, and plump lobes merged into an elastic mass of flesh, a hunk of meat that slapped and wobbled in the tray.

The outer glaze of the lungs lost its lustre as the sun went behind the woods, filling the classroom with bleak shadow, and his treatment of the lungs became rougher: turning them this way and that, a puppet to his dictatorship. The initial fascination with the lungs waned as learning became routine. Eyes drifted away, unrelated conversation began. It was either the lungs themselves or the methods by which Mr Stephens was teaching that led to the growing lack of attention, but I remember how my own mind wandered away from the specimen to the original vessel of life in which it was housed and given real animation, the blood pumping through, hot and quick, powering the animal as it breathed in summer dawn air, snuffled the mud, pressing leaves into the ground as it ran. The absence of the animal haunted the lungs like a phantom limb, a stolen fragment of a whole life. How old was the animal? Where did it thrive, feed, and drink? What was its story? I did not even ask what animal the lungs belonged to. It wouldn't have been relevant.

The class bustled out of the room at the strike of the bell. I lingered at the back, turning at the door to see what Mr Stephens would do with the lungs. He toppled them into a bright yellow plastic bag like the ones I had seen in surgery theatres, twirled the bag closed and tied a double knot, then rinsed the tray in the deep white sink in the shadowy far corner of the room.

My walk home took me through a cemetery and I thought about those lungs, and about my own, disturbed that I had an organ like that working within me, growing and shrinking with each breath.

A lone grave beside the footpath had recently been garlanded with flowers: a rainbow of tulips secured together at the ends of their stalks by a fist-size stone. The headstone was a thick marble book, open, etched with the name of the buried in elongated italics, half of the letters weathered away, the dates registering a time before I was born. I stopped at the grave's edge. A balmy wind brushed high hedgerows, children played in hidden gardens, a male blackbird fluttered out from a tattered yew, shot low straight down the corridor of headstones, then alighted with a slight dip of his tail upon the ground. Standing there, my hands in my pockets, I slowly became aware, in some dim and deep-down way, of stories taking shape without words, each connected by white threads floating through the air, glinting on the verge of invisibility like gossamer slivers of spiderweb blown by the wind across the sun. And these stories were the shapes of bodies I had never seen before, filled with eagerness and waiting, shifting containers of energy fleetingly embroidered by the threads that moved from one body to the other like the passing touch of a mother's warm hand across the cheek of her waking child before she throws open the curtains, letting in the light. Where this 'vision' was happening I couldn't tell for sure but it seemed to rise out from a space between me and the surroundings, not in a violent rupture but in a seamless interruption of one moment's association with the next.

The Stone Wall

Shepherd, daily you decline my helping hand
to restore the old stone wall around your farm.

A crow is pecking out an injured ewe's eyes,
tearing her teats that spill milk into the mud.
Her lamb is crying out from the mountain.
The cuckoo's flute is out of tune.

You bare your toothless grin
while sparring with an open fire, peeling back moleskins
with your thumbnail as though they were
black, deformed potatoes.

An adder's skin floats by on the wind.
Swallows, nattering and defecating upon your gable end,
will die in their nests you stuff full with poison.

Snowdon is a god keeping a watchful eye
upon your dour, pebble-dash house – an igloo of rust –
swallowed by waves of diesel, bracken and sprockets.

Dog chains rattle in the rainfall of night.
Big Bear crouches over your sleeping mare.

Look, Shepherd, your son is moping back from school,
scuffing his feet through a desert of gravel,
munching broken biscuits of slate, gargling soot.

At night, you wake to the screams of his night terrors. In a gown of bandages and barbed wire, you limp outside and fire your shotgun at dark winged figures breathing heavily in the trees.

Living in the Shadow of the Rain

The Black Lamb

A black lamb lay dead upon the flank of Raven Mountain.[1]
A fist-size head twisted up towards the higher rocks. Splayed
legs pointing limply down to low fields. A thin gash around
its waist seeped blood and rain into grasses tugged this way
and that by the wind. One raven drew dark circles around
the sky, croaking like the old joints of granite rock. Stepping
over the lamb, I walked up into the wind to the stone wall
that threaded the throat of the summit. Heather deeply
seethed whilst grasses deeply whispered. Rain in flashes
burst by, crashing against my coat, flying through the valley
towards other mountains, other valleys.

Down in the valley at the field's edge, a dark figure
strode over asphalt from a house greyer than the clouds,
and colder to look at, to the sheep pen. He moved with
ease against the wind and rain as he unlatched the gate
and kicked the black ewes free into the field to scatter. In
the field, black lambs whined as the mothers searched for
their own. The figure leaned attentively over the gate,
watching. Another figure, a small blur, ran out of the house
and stood beside him. Father and son. One mother ewe
stumbled back and forth, bleating, calling, over the stone-
pocked field. No lamb bounded to her. Father and son
watched on, the boy's chin resting on folded hands holding
the gate's top bar. The mother covered all corners of the

---

[1] Raven Mountain is not the actual name of the mountain in this story.
Out of privacy, its actual name, like the names of the father and son, has
not been used.

field, searching, running as father and son drifted back into the house through strengthening wind and rain. I could hear her gargled scream as she stood amongst other mothers matched to their own lambs. Coming down from the summit to the stone wall I spooked two ravens from the dead lamb, which, when I leaned over it, was punctured and torn, its eyes gone, leaving two shocking holes, the waist gash a rip right through its stomach that spilled organs into mud. The ravens' beaks gleamed as they watched me from a silver birch like two statues carved from Whitby jet. I wondered if the dead lamb belonged to the bereft ewe.

Lambs and frantic mothers approached, stomped, and then ran away as I walked through their stronghold, hopping the ladder stile. The porch of the grey house was dark like a cliff cave, and littered with coal overspilling the coal bunker. Two chunks crushed into black dust under my heel and soaked into the rain that streamed from the gutters, pooling at two empty doghouses crowned with rusted chains. The dark door opened after my knocks and a man filled the doorway, wearing a long anorak like a soaked shadow. A boy loomed up from under his thick arm, wearing a red woollen hat that frowned his brow to his eyes. Old heat wafted out from the brightly lit interior of the house. I told him about the black lamb. The door gently closed on me after a string of sarcastic words were left dangling like hooks in the air.

From the porch, the desert of asphalt was dark, stretching away towards my lodgings, and the rain, in wind-hurled gusts, skittered off the fine stones to crash in waves against the dingy house that seemed to be made from the mountain itself.

The wind and rain boomed as I lay in my bed facing the midnight profile of Raven Mountain. I drifted to sleep to the dream-sounds of the ravens croaking over their meal, to the stare of the man in the doorway – the bones of his face emerging through his skin like the brown-grey branches and roots of heather, the eyes chiselled from stone, and the warmth of his breath like the mouldy heat of the house – and to the bud of the boy's life on the brink of twisting in or out of shape beneath the watch of the father. The arm around the boy's throat like a shepherd's crook.

The Dark Pool

I toed the water's edge of the dark March river, the smooth sleeve of its berm running and riding up around my ankles, the water leaving traces of liquid bracelets. A crow flurried up from an island, a stick in its bill.

The son took me to swim in the river that still bore the traumas of winter's grip, the white knuckles of ice jamming the spouts and the narrow grooves. I had never swum in such freezing water and yet the son, stripped bare, his skin freckled and wrapped in goosebumps, kneeled his way into the give of the pool that was pale-dark at its outer rim and, through increasingly dark concentric ripples, black at its centre. The son slogged out and swam as a son of the water, grinning. From an iron bridge that spanned the Stygian pool he leapt as I, a timid spectator, stood by. He urged me to take the leap but I wouldn't. He knew the river well and where the underneath rocks lay. He jumped again, and emerged back up from the deep water. Before he had even looked up at the bridge I was making my way down.

Daffodils

Spring was slothful, and at first winter wouldn't leave, returning every few days to gather any last lost garments, but it left for good as it finally allowed the snowdrops to erupt. Daffodils echoed the sun.

The father gathered daffodils for his son with the creased crook of his hand, bending low along the lane's edge, tearing them mid-stalk, the ragged edge seeping the gluey sap that glinted in the sun. Sweet translucent blood on his calloused hand. The son accepted them, and the father pinned one golden head to his school blazer, close to the heart. The rest he lay down on the wall, a bouquet for the wind to dandle, an offering to Raven Mountain, and left. The son waited on the lane for the school bus, now and again nodding down to glance at the daffodil.

He returned home in the afternoon, hopped off the bus at the bridge that spanned the black river fumbled by fallen oaks, the daffodil head flopping up and down on his blazer. He walked up from the bus stop to the house, first reaching the dogs that barked, snarled, and trembled, their chains rattling, their yelps echoing off the cliffs of Raven Mountain; he ran his milk-white hands through the decaying bouquet the father had left on the wall. Two daffodils had fallen to the ground, crossing in an X. Three others were battered through by the cold teeth of the wind nibbling at them all day.

Taking Flight

House martins trickled down from the eaves of my home. Two swallows had returned to their scrappy nests under the fire escape. Their red throats, like brandings from the Saharan scorch, quaked as they screeched their scratchy rapid songs, and their bodies shook as they called to one another on the telegraph wire. They swooped down the alleyways and corkscrewed into the blue sky towards the sun.

The father's house was also decked with the nests of swallows and house martins – those little dirt and spit cups crafted to endure the turns in weather and cradle the newborn and the fledglings. He emerged from the dark cavern of his garage holding a bulging sack of rat poison. Stacking up a ladder beneath the eaves, he moved with the diligence of a surveyor from nest to nest, spooning rat poison into the warm, dark holes. And the swallows and house martins flew in and out of the nests, their beaks lined with a neon-green slime.

He hated the mess they made, I heard him say to a visitor, hated the way they shat over the drainpipes.

Days later I held a dead house martin in my hands as he and his son patrolled the field, pressing shotguns down into molehills, waiting for blind eyes to nuzzle kindly into the May air. The house martin's head, like a paper-made skull, lopped over the thumb of my cupped hand, her wings wet with rain and frozen stiff. Wooden and thin, she brushed my palm as she rolled from my outstretched hand with the lightness of the last touch of soil around a newly planted bulb.

I put her into the evening bonfire I had lit to consume the pine boards of a demolished shed. She was sucked into the raging flame, which spurted up in a flurry of sparks that searched to and fro. The florid orange flames licked her poisoned bones. A wild cremation. The shadows of the fire danced upon the wall of the shepherd's house.

The Cormorant

I had been out on the marshes since dawn. The seethe of wind through bouncing reeds held me listening and looking for a while longer before I reached for the car door. A single lapwing flapped overhead, pouncing from one wing to the other, flying east to re-enter big flocks I had watched earlier in the day sky-dance above Normandy Lagoon. Their Morse-code call was still eeping in my ears along with the glug-slap of the Solent against the sea wall, the chorus behind all the day's sights and sounds.

Scythe-like, a stronger wind bluntly swung through the reeds that bordered Avon Water where, at that spot by the car, it churned in a weir beneath Illey Lane and rolled out into Keyhaven Harbour. Swans turned tail first in the swirling froth. Overhead, clouds interlocked to form a pewter sheet of April sky, and bruised themselves on impact.

There was something flapping at the edge of the lane beside the river, like a black bin bag fluttering in the wind. It was a cormorant. I stuffed my car keys in my pocket, rested my binoculars on the car roof, and approached her, my sounds swallowed by the noise of the weir and the wind.

She tried to scurry away, her right wing flopping into the river, and she was almost dragged into the weir gate. I cupped my hands around her chest from behind and gently pulled her back up onto the mudbank, her webbed feet leaving a trail of helplessness. There was no doubt that she was terrified of me, seeing me as a shape of offensive threat, the shadow of death. But she was stuck in her pain, forced to endure the end of her life and the presence of mine. She gargled. Her head lolled to the side over the arch between my finger and thumb as though I had strangled, not cradled her. As her smooth, jet-black head fell with its flint bill, I met her prehistoric eye. Its implacability was mesmerising. Its remote gaze, like an eye before time, allured me to return the stare. I was taken in by a look that, as it drew me towards it, cut through me with a precision matched only by the keen edge of her bill. Forged for air and sea, elements in which I am only a momentary visitor, her eye cauterised where it struck through. A pearl-blue iris, splintered with gold, spoked out from a ball-bearing black pupil, and a cornea so vividly green the colour was not a mere quality but a dynamic constituent of the bird, like blood, oxygen. It was like looking through a microscope into an aurora borealis, in an exquisite restless synergy, congealing into an iron stare that swelled with a stringent preciousness as her breathing faltered to a wheeze, her whole body letting go of itself. Glassy, yes, but not like a mirror or window. I did not see myself in her eyes. Nor, I guess, did she see herself in mine. There was no marriage of creatures to one another, no atonement. There was only this charge of energy that was, in that moment, essential. My hands released their grip from her salt-roughened vanes, her cold feathers. She gasped, collapsed in a heap of honeycomb bones. Her wings splayed, the electricity of her soaring eye quivered like a light flickering out in the far room of a strange house surrounded by wind-blown reeds.

I ran to the pub and retrieved a Walkers Crisps box from the barman, who was, though thrown off guard, obliging about my request. I gathered up the bird in a woollen-cloud of Welsh blanket that my mum and dad had bought from Snowdonia before I was born, and lowered her into the box, into the boot of my car. She sank deeper and deeper into the midnight cot of her impending death as I held my breath, it seemed, all the way to the veterinary clinic at Lymington, careering around the corners of Illey Lane, breathing again as I passed her into a stranger's hands over a counter in a brightly lit foyer. The vet's eyes, her half-smile, her outstretched hands, were gestures of reassurance. After taking the box, the bird, she gracefully handed me the checked blanket, which I rolled around my right forearm. Heavy rain lashed across the car park. I draped the blanket over the back seat as neatly as I could.

Khami Metals

Prince was almost as big as a lion. His paws dwarfed my own hands. His bark could be heard above the clanging din of the yard, a clipped and thunderous yap. Prince was the Alsatian guard dog at Granddad's yard. Secured in a pen the size of a horse stable, snug against the towering main gate of corrugated steel topped with rolls of razor wire, Prince's was the first face you would see on entering the yard. He was stationed there all night, to protect the place. Back home, I would think of him alone with nothing but the eerie stillness and silence of sleeping machines and hills of metal glowing in the moonlight or in the rain that formed ponds of run-off in the gullies, rainwater and diesel coagulating to form rainbow sheens in the day. I turned cold when I imagined that he was cold. I slept in a curled-up ball as he would have done, the night air saturated with the reek of diesel.

Now and again he was allowed to run and sniff freely amongst the hills of steel, cars, aluminium bales, cocking his leg up on machines, staining their sides with shadow-splashes of pee. He left his mark throughout the yard. You could always tell where he roamed by tracking his paw marks in the thick and slick mud, amongst the tyre ruts and boot prints. It was like searching for the last traces of an animal in an industrial apocalypse. The workers liked him too, but if you looked into his coal-black eyes for too long he would lift his quivering lips and bare his gums and the points of his teeth. And sometimes he would give you a shallow nip on the calf to remind you of his presence. It made me laugh when, sneaking up behind a worker busily absorbed in running wire through the wire-cutter, he would nip the man's heel and then, rather than scampering, would confront the man, who, shocked, clasped his heel and cursed.

When Granddad and Dad returned to England after fifteen years of trading metal in Botswana, mostly selling the disused parts of railways as they underwent regeneration, they brought with them their business name – Khami Metals – and set up a twenty-acre plot on the outskirts of Basingstoke. Two Saturdays or so a month we would go to Khami Metals as a whole family. By then I was old enough. It also meant we got to see Dad throughout the weekend. Saturday was only a half-day, too, and much less hectic than the rest of the working week. My brother and I were free to explore and I spent most of the morning playing with Prince. With a sudden flood of raucous customers eager to cash in on their collections for the weekend, the yard turned into a rally course of forklifts zipping back and forth, and lorries beeping as they manoeuvred and reversed onto the weighbridge. I would sit beside Prince's pen showing him bits and pieces I discovered in the yard, and fed him food I stole from name-labelled Tupperware crammed in the office fridge. His big nose would press hard against a brass bolt I found, smelling it with such strength it was as if he was trying to extract every smidgen of colour and texture from it.

When a modern alarm system was finally implemented in the yard, Prince was no longer needed, and found a new home at a family farm near Winchester. I wasn't given any warning when I walked through the main gate one Saturday in the half-dark, expecting to see his face, to hear his heavy tail thwacking the sides of his pen, to find instead that he wasn't there. But Mum was right in saying he would be much happier on a farm. It was cruel to keep him locked up here, she said. That consoled me. But I found it hard to imagine that he wouldn't miss me. From then on I missed him during those Saturdays. I missed losing my hands in the deep warmth of his dusky-golden fur; a necessary contact of softness amidst the harsh chaos of metal and machines. I missed our silent conversations in his quiet corner. I even went hunting for his last remaining paw print until it was squashed and erased by the track wheel of the crane. Soon, his empty pen became a storehouse for boxes, computer boards, rats, used gloves, and empty drums of Swarfega.

My brother and I began to spend more time wreaking havoc in the yard. The workers called us 'nippers'. Dad and Mum, overwhelmed by work, would leave us unattended. We began to know the landscape of Khami Metals intimately. Now that I attached myself to my older brother, the twingeing absence of Prince became less immediate, far less acute. Dad would hand us both sledgehammers – although it took both of us to lift one of them – and we were free to swing at demolished cars, their parts removed, their hoods crumpled, ready to be rolled into the pit baler, to be crushed into a cube. Or we rode the stationary forklifts, turning their wheels in spasm-like jolts, mimicking the sounds and movements of a high-speed car chase.

Sometimes Dad, during a respite in the seemingly endless train of work, escorted us to the back of the yard, to the most dangerous parts. Here, two cranes swung grabs that opened out like gigantic arthritic tarantulas, piercing through cars with serene and murderous fortitude, lifting them high, tossing them up onto the ridge of the car mountain. The crane driver, aloft in his cabin in the skies, controlled the beast like the brain. They worked in tandem. The grabs whooshed through the air with daunting power and speed. Spiders flying, weaving webs of demolition, assembling caches of prey. Then the desiccated car, nonchalantly chosen by the grab, was flicked into the pit like a discarded pistachio shell. The pit was barricaded from us by a three-metre-high fence. Through its cracks I could see the edge of the abyss, and a glimpse of the darkness within, the crane feeding the bowels of the yard, a voracious sinkhole. If we were caught here on our own, my brother and I, then we got locked up in the office for the remainder of the day with Mum, surrounded by high, leaning stacks of invoice boxes. It was dark and dusty in the office. Mum tried to keep it as tidy as possible, but, by her next visit, papers always littered the floor, spilling out of brown boxes with splitting sides, a ray of sunlight choked wan by unswept dust.

Dad said he once saw a man fall into the baler pit. Whether it was true or not, it came as a warning and filled me with fear. As the jaws of the baler squeezed the car into a disc, then revolved it into a cube the size of a domestic wheelie bin, the ground reverberated like an earthquake. Very occasionally, Dad took us up into the cabin of the crane. It was like scaling a mountain, the rungs of the built-in ladder stretching far below and the horizon of the distant countryside opening out beyond, a wind starting up and blowing across us. I could almost see home. Once, when we were in the cabin, the grab swung back like a pendulum, hurtling, almost crashing into us. I was terrified and clung on to Dad. I was amazed by his dexterity with the levers and gears, and how calmly he commanded the colossal machine. I began to gain a sense of what he did all day.

The Hut

Dominic, recall the collapsing Nissen hut
draped in slack lengths of army canvas.
Blue tarpaulin billowing in the wind.

Inside: rusted parts of a butcher's bike,
soil from a roe's hoof, the badger's foil,
asbestos snowing upon nuts and bolts.

Outside: the nagging of our mothers
to come inside. The cupboards, the fluids,
the empty plastic utensils of their home.

Our friendship found its own abode
where living things would bud and glow
to fix the bond tighter in downpours

of harshly angled rain. The roof drumming.
The hut standing upon a wild lawn of awe.
The horizons shifting with every shift in our eyes.

Border of Light

The Horse's Kick

I am standing alone in the drab cream kitchen of student halls — the air sultry and reeking of bleach, spilled garbage, stains of old alcohol — holding the back of a dimpled, blue plastic chair, looking out of a smeary window onto a building site. Mounds of rubble like massive molehills darken in these Thursday-afternoon drifts of emulsion rain. The nasal rumble of a drill is the sound of a headache.

I am trying hard not to roil in a sinking pit of homesickness when my mum calls to say you were flung from your horse, your head kicked in on your way down. Fractures to a tender skull, internal bleeding. I hear the wincing thud of your fall in Mum's voice, and close my eyes. She says mine was the first name you called out as, thrashing as though that horse still lay upon you, immovable, you fretfully emerged from a three-day coma into the sterile glow of a hospital room where, around your bed in a circular link of strenuous, prayerful waiting, your mum, dad, and two sisters enwreathed themselves.

I have not seen nor have I spoken to you in a decade, and yet you call out my name upon the steep intersecting verges of life and death. After school years we diverted down separate paths from a childhood of shared adventures that I had almost — until this bolt of rupturing news — forgotten. I have to get home to see you, those fields, that farm, to be of meaning, freed from the emptiness of here, the ruined view, this stench.

I think of you now. Our friendship was founded by your family's land and your claim upon it. I looked to you as the leader into the bloodlines of love that met down amongst the grasses by the barns, beside the sea of fields, where your mother tended her horses and your father dug ditches to drain away floods.

Adopted into revelry for the pauses between birdsong and the warmth of newly laid eggs and the summer hideaways of the dark barns, I was given a space to belong beside you and your family around the meal of the earth, the plates piled high with twigs and stars. The hungers were satisfied. Never was it a struggle to be at home in the world. Belonging was the air we breathed.

You took me in and together we planted the flag of innocence sewn from eager wonder for the unfenced skies. That deep green flag still blows now, down by the hedgerow upon the shining field. The wielding axes of time have yet to fell it. I hear it billowing in my hours of need for a richer and more humble treatment of this wild green home of earth.

Children take the smallest steps and yet have the largest stride of any human heart. Like water, nothing else necessary but themselves. You and I were two creatures of the elements, moving at ease between air and fire, our lungs and the rising sun. Without words we took an oath to each other before the eyes of the land. And too soon that oath is broken when the demands of growing up put a heavy hand upon us and, overnight, we cannot move as swiftly as we did. The heaviness seems a hefty price to pay for doing everything right.

And yet I swear, in the eyes of the land once again if she is still watching, to lose this heaviness. My past with you is not a burden but a remedy. It lifts me up into the arms of the earth. And so I swear to never lose sight of that stream which trickled around the back of the far fields, the stream that I could cross now in a single leap but, back then, forded as through a mighty bull-headed river, dragging my pole net that glistened with watery beads of shivering light and jumping silver minnows.

That small world of stream, field, barn, and hedgerows was big beyond measure. Our hearts were discovered there. Adults grip maps that constrict the land, but our world was dilated. A grass blade was at once a support for a star and the hair upon the field's body. The fields, the barn, the sky, were bigger under each sun. Maps, measurements, metres – these are ailments of the inverted eye, when innocence is lost.

I will never lose the sense of that which is close, near, being the most spacious. The particulars have always been more than enough. It is a truth that we lived back then; now we must go through pains to prove it. Our sight deteriorates with age, but that doesn't have to be the case. The near is all. Friends and family diverge and cross in a million and one ways. What is close is where the close ones live. Leaves stuffed up our sleeves, our separate hands folded around the same branch, hanging upside down with the tops of our heads freezing tight in the ale-brown stream.

The Visit

During the pauses of our disjointed conversation, the ticks of the white clock upon the chalk-blue wall of your bedroom are repeated announcements that we are now living in a broken world with no covenants of reparation. We do not know what to do with where the present has brought us. We have nowhere, it seems, to speak from. It is as though the childhood we shared here is a figment of some other's imagination. But as your mum warned me when I tentatively knocked at the front door, put one foot upon the first stair, holding the bannister, leaning forward in preparation for the climb up the oak stairs to your bedroom, the blow to your head by the horse induced memory loss, amnesia.

It is as though you only half recognise me now. Have I changed that much? Why shout out my name? The scar from the hoof runs from the top of your skull into a down-sloping curve to your left temple, an inch above your ear. The stitches are rough and sharp, like a track of barbs. Your patchy hair is faded to a plaster-grey where the line of the hefty wound runs. I trail my fingers over the stitching and the absence between us begins to dissolve. You bring your head away from under my lingering right hand, then run your own fingers up the scar, your eyes widening, your fingertips staying, in gentle disbelief, touching what I touched in an anointment of yourself, blessed to be alive. I am getting close to the life we shared, the warmth of it. Memories flood in. We begin to reminisce, to weave patterns of connection between us. Such talk, though, does not go without strain. The horse that struck you is close by still, breathing hard, trapped somewhere between your heart and mine, its chest expanding and contracting. I hear that horse in everything you say, its hooves drumming the ground more loudly than the clock on the wall.

Leaving for Nowhere

By early evening you are drained. Your eyelids teeter under the wakeful strain of conversation. Your hazel eyes, maroon-green in their deepest part, lose lustre under the power of oncoming sleep.

Outside, the farm withdraws into shadow. The day's sharp edges of clearly demarcated fields, silhouettes of barns, variegated fences – posts, railings, and hedges – surrender their definition and meld into the thickening flood of darkness, the bringer of dreams. Final clucks of exasperated hens as they shuffle and jive up chipboard ramps into coops, the last grunting whines of goats, the salient purring of a nightjar. I wonder, if we were to stay up through the night, whether the fox of our past would appear at its unearthly hour.

Inside, the house's plumbing creaks like barn hinges, the radiators gargle. You feel the cold mostly at night, you say, even when the heating is on full. You rock back, away from me, and lie down upon your side facing the wall as though an invisible pair of hands encourage and guide your body to rest. Your arms hold one another and slide underneath your right cheek into the mercy of the pillow. I think of the soft thrumming of the pulse in your temple that, because you were such a light sleeper, would keep you awake at night.

I am surprised how much you have remembered today despite the loss of memory the horse induced. The clock returns, exclaiming itself like a nocturnal pest of every night. The hallway light frames the bedroom door with a glow as your mum cautiously opens it. A border of light. My visit is over. To keep you from your sleep would be cruel. We neither hug nor shake hands. I let you lie.

The silence in the room tastes faintly like iron, like blood. I carry anguish and beneficence like stones and feathers in the pockets of my tattered Barbour jacket as I step past your mum, who half smiles in mild sorrow, drop down into the orange light of the hallway, and descend the stairs one by one. The front door has not changed. Once I was small enough to press my forehead directly upon the brass door handle, and stare through the letter box to see you running towards me from the kitchen, skidding on socks that stretched beyond your toes.

The house, the outbuildings, the fields, and the woods beyond, shape a revenant farewell in the evening dark beneath an overcast sky wounded, here and there, by the hoof prints of the stars. Brilliant lesions. Your bedroom light is out. The horse that prints the stars is galloping between eternity and time, through landscapes of innocence and loss, searching, searching.

Tadpoles

Amy, you should've spent your life guarding
tadpoles from herons, people, and drought.
At every step on our walk to Llyn Crafnant
you stop to scrutinise puddles peppered

with tadpole eggs, clogged with spawn
wobbling under your pronounced thickness test.
We walk so slowly to give you time but time
sloughs away and you shrink into a child again

in yellow wellingtons speckled with mud,
happiest on your own, missing your minor
part in a play because you're outside peering
down the microscope of a well at tadpoles.

Or you're in your father's garden collecting them
in jam jars, giving each one a cartoon name,
roles for plumbers, artists, nuns and gymnasts,
selecting the best to exhibit on shining sills.

I disappear entirely from your day until your
tired eyes need the path ahead. You catch up
with time that's preciously waited, like me, to witness
your sudden wriggling spurt into adulthood.

The Metolius River

For 'Seed', our little body of life, lost to a missed miscarriage at five weeks.

We took the long road south, gazing out west towards the snowy peak of Mount Jefferson, letting our eyes roll away with Oregon's golden grasslands. Bald eagles sailed overhead, unfolding their bodies from lone and disused fence posts, kicking up with nonchalant power, beating their broad wings with enthralling surety, casting shadows like clouds above our turning heads.

Stopping at a deep gorge of pocked basalt, the Deschutes River a glinting thread of noiseless water at the bottom, we watched a man fall from the iron bridge on a purple bungee rope, screaming till he came to a gut-crunching halt. He dangled by his heels way down, a speck encircled by a pair of golden eagles whose calls echoed throughout the gorge with ringing sharpness. The noon sun was intense, every detail of the gorge was match-struck by the clarity of the sunlight.

Amy had been feeling fatigued for a week or so and was anxious to know why. She seemed withdrawn even though she was animated by the magnificence of the scenes. She had been suffering from headaches, from nausea. When we arrived in Sisters later that afternoon, jaded from the journey, we parked up outside our bunkhouse. She went straight to a pharmacy, and back in the room the pregnancy test showed positive. We had been trying for so long. Our lives, suddenly, clicked into a new place that transcended and included all that had gone before in our relationship. It was as though the roof had been blown off and we could see a sky so beautiful that tears brimmed in our eyes.

I had never given much thought to how I would react, what feelings would arise, to the sense of preparation for the future, the identity of becoming a father, a dad. What had I learned from my father and how would I incorporate that in the sense of my own self, whoever in fact I was? Did I know myself well enough to know I could be a good father? A confusion of considerations, but the joy was the thing, the joy of having deepened and expanded our love for one another to the point where, in a wordless way, life made sense.

Amy took the test again, to make sure. The heavy fatigue that had cloaked her for the past week could now be explained. We embraced as though we had found one another after a long absence.

I had read about the Metolius River. With its name coming from the Sahaptin *mit' 'ula*, meaning 'spawned-out salmon' – the beginning and the end of the salmon's journey – it seemed that the river was meant for us. It was all the more important now to seek it out, to walk its banks, to hear and touch its flow, to round off that afternoon with the blessedness of water and stone and light, to share our news with the river in which the wild salmon spawned.

The bunkhouse owner, whose enthusiasm for the Metolius was contagious, pointed us in the right direction. After a brief drive further north, we arced left through a high pine forest that shared out the late-afternoon sunlight in uniform arrangements upon the forest floor and onto other trees, then slowed down the car at Camp Sherman, hearing the gush of the river before the ignition was cut, hearing the flow before we could see it. We held hands as we walked together to the river's bank and looked upon the water.

The river sang as it pulsed, eddied, and flowed onwards, marrying with the surrounding scent of pine. The stones shone beneath the surface, some as round as watch faces, smoothed by aeons of kneading, with curved edges that glinted and shimmered in their beds of sticks and chalk-white sand. The water was so clear that the stones were without shadows, big, bright, and full-coloured. Branches and grasses overhanging the surface were doubled upon the water, replicated exactly and preciously aligned. We both knelt down on the low bank between grasses and touched the cold water with our fingertips.

An osprey double-backed over the river, its talons aimed down towards the water, the shadow of that bird fleeing across the surface. We looked up at the bird, and beyond it at the blue of the Oregon sky.

A mile or so further south, a small group of grassy islands tufted with bowing rushes were home to a family of otters that rolled and splashed in the water, their slick fur oiled with light. They hadn't seen us. In silence we watched on, six metres or so from the otters as they plunged and rose with comfort and sleekness. The water rushed over them as they settled upon one of three logs that created a natural pool in a deep bend away from the river's central course. They loped and fell over one another, mother harassed by three pups slapping their feet along the bald log then over her as though she was a ramp.

They took off and crumpled silently into the water to hunt or play.

We sat there until the osprey passed overhead again, an hour or so from when it last appeared, towards the three peaks of Sisters, their snowy tops like still, sunlit summer clouds just glimpsed through the dense pine wood. We had no aim but to amble, not to see what we could find but what might catch us off guard. I walked barefoot, my boots slung around my neck. Now and again I stopped and tilted my head up into the warmth of the sun, closing my eyes.

Alone on the warm path, we entered a dense wood of ponderosa pine, their old needles carpeting the forest floor, their bark rough to the touch and cracked like riven tiles. The silence of the wood overcame us as the sunlight faded over the Cascade mountains, and the crisp outlines of the trees soon began to blur with the onset of dusk. Regretfully, we left the river behind, still hearing its wash and the occasional reverberating *glop* of stones collapsing along the riverbed, the sound shuddering through the air and through the earth.

Before we headed back to Sisters along Highway 22, we drove from Camp Sherman to the visible source of the Metolius, the birth of that magical and majestic river within a deep chamber of Black Butte. On the short drive there we talked of the river's beauty, the animals we had seen, and of Amy's pregnancy, the new life beginning within her.

At its source, the river seemed as essential as love and as ancient and virile as the living earth. I sensed its life, the life it supports, its nourishing mystery. I felt drawn into it, wanted it to hold our child too, accepting and trusting in its power without hesitation as though it were a kind of love.

Except for our breathing the only sound in the darkening woods was from the springs in the mountainside. Water volleyed forth from a green cleft of fern- and moss-draped rock, and ruptured up to the surface in exploded globes. It was from this collection of springs that the Metolius grew, its turbulent length eventually joining the Deschutes River twenty-nine miles away to the south. I crouched low over the cold water and hovered my hand above the bubbling cauldron. It was mesmerising. Amy came down to join me. We stared together into the lifeblood of the river, the site of its visible birth gathered and released from somewhere deep within the earth like all mysteries, like all wonders. The birth of an element. We watched the Metolius being born, refreshed, and reborn in a miraculous continuation of explosions, eddies, whirls, and flows.

Falling into accord with the movement of that afternoon river was not an alien sensation but rather a comfortable entanglement with two lovers carefully bearing their feelings for one another in a world that, at times, seems to work against love. Things came together along that river. By the time our attention slackened the high pines were wraith-like silhouettes and the spaces between the pines were dark and wide.

Back at the bunkhouse, full of sleep, our conversation was made up of two spellbinding threads: the Metolius River and the seed of life that was growing in Amy.

Summer

Swifts

Happy again, the swifts are back
in acrobatic aerial war
along the cliff's slumped ridge,
arrowing down narrow Becton,
simmering their reflections
upon the brown waters of Natterjack,
spinning down Dilly Lane
where you, Father,
Father, you stand stupefied
by the beauty of their flock,
amazed that they can sleep on the wing hurtling,
that a scattering sinew of earth
can still return with equal vigour,
and I, Father, I am in there somewhere
or miles behind at the path's start
trying to get to you,
so wait,
wait for me,
and together we can fear the Hobby,
how its bolt leaves a bruise in the blue,
a flash of underwing,
its dodging of wrong thermals
for the right one it will love and soar
that will throw him straight
into the Swift's heart.

But we, Father,
we have the one time to get it right,
to hit the red target and remain there.

The Fox of the Unearthly Hour

Once, in this very room, we stayed up all through a summer week night waiting for the fox of the unearthly hour. Do you remember?

We huddled close beneath a hide of bedsheets strung from the bedposts on one side of the room across to the desk legs on the other, rationing snacks and half-pints of full-fat milk. Putting fingers clenched into tight cylinders to our eyes as if using binoculars, resting our chins on the cool, cushion-lined window sill, we watched, staring, waiting, never wavering. Around 4 a.m. our wonder was rewarded. The fox stepped out from a dark blackberry bush, then placidly trotted towards the centre of the moonlit field, paused and blazed fiery-white like an animal Roman candle, its hectic shadow flickering across fields, in our eyes, until its effervescence subsided. It shook white sparks out from its amber fur, then slunk off towards the high barn, ducked, and disappeared from our sight behind rickety towers of haystacks that held up the star-frescoed dome of the night sky. Our breath steamed the window. We pulled our hands away from our eyes, placed them flat on the sill, our fingers aching after holding them in circles for so long. We did not sleep a wink that night. Our eyes on fire did not close, our corneas branded with the incandescent fox.

The encounter was worth every minute of fatigue at school the next day. We looked across the row of desks at one another with a sense of devious privilege that we shared a secret no one else could believe, their heads busily nodding in repressed panic at the corrective methods of the mathematics teacher as she scribbled equation after equation upon the flat board. The neatly configured lines of numbers made no sense to me. The fox had no place here. The image of that fox spluttering into white flames fizzed in my mind. The teacher was wasting her time with me, with us.

We laugh as we recall that we fell asleep in class, your smile now a mirror image of the smile in that classroom across the desks. This was the learning I cherished: the resonance of inscrutable lives. We shared a world where maths could not pry, where the fox was at home in the blaze of its belonging. I thank you for this. Between laughs, you run your fingers over your scar.

A Nest for the Dream Bird

We built a nest for a bird that didn't exist. 'Dream Bird', we called it. We drew it first, untidily, again and again, trying to get it right, an image born of two minds, tense cooperation. White paper sheets carpeted the grass. Crayons crumbled. Our final collaborated vision was this: a bloated, elongated kingfisher with a stubby bill like a chaffinch, legs like sticks of charcoal with serrated crow's feet splayed out. Wings golden emerald, eyes like raspberry moons. And it could fly at the speed of sound, higher than the clouds, and burrow like a mole into earth for grubs, worms, roots. Its call, we deduced, was a symphony of squawks rounded with a buzzard's mew but more angelic, finished with a last trill that was deafening. It could be heard for miles around. And its body was always warm even when snow clung to its smooth feathers and rain ruffled it to double its size. It belonged to no one, not even us, the ingenious inventors of fresh life, child gods without a care in the world except this one project.

A home fitting for its uniqueness was the next trial. Making life was hard enough, let alone a nest to match its worth. We dug out a cereal-sized bowl in the ground by hand, grappling with increasingly cold and wet layers of earth. Our fingers met worms of all sizes: thumb-fat, spaghetti-thin and long, some as straight as straws, or inflated like sausage balloons, blotched pink and pale red like the flushed skin of embarrassment. These worms were the food cache, put to one side in a makeshift larder, a writhing pile contained in a box of twigs and leaves no bigger than your pocket-money bank. The Dream Bird's stash, a gift from us, an offering. Your mum brought us sandwiches and juice, which we ate and glugged with hands stiffened by mud drying in the sun of summer. Your golden retrievers pawed the cool pocket of earth, and inspected the worms with wet noses.

Once the round hole was completed, we carefully chose nest linings for the Dream Bird's needs – not too warm otherwise the bird would wilt like a flower, and not too sparsely stuffed otherwise it would attract ice that would contract around it like arthritis. Moss, mainly, torn from the edge of a lawn across the road; golden fur gathered from your dogs; feathers shed from your geese and ducks. And more moss from the barn roof, sheared off with spades whilst we balanced on rusty ladders, ungainly as thieves on stilts. We made the nest sturdy to last through the tests of time, and soft for the bird's preciousness. It was perfect.

Then we waited and waited behind a hedge for the Dream Bird's arrival. Our waiting was a summoning, a prayer. From our sketch to the sky we looked and looked, our hearts beating in our heads. The space around us ripening for the bird's entrance from dream into reality, the nest the centre of its world. The all-day absence of it was as enthralling as its expected presence. Until our patience snapped. And we jaunted off to make something else: rods and reels for the minnows in the tan-brown stream. They were an easy catch compared to our Dream Bird.

The Stag

Summer ferns were shoulder-high in Bolderwood, in the New Forest, even head-high around the sun-dappled rim of the clearing where our class, taken there on a school trip, assembled. We were separated into pairs and allotted two hours to build the best camps we could. I cannot remember what the prize was.

I worked with a girl whose blonde hair sparkled in the sun, flowing down around her shoulders, falling to her lower back. Moss, tacky sticks caught in it every time she kneeled down to gather material for our camp. Her hair brushed over dead leaves, each strand a fibre of gold braided by canopy-caught rays.

Our camp resembled a lopsided tepee scaffolded with rotten sticks and roofed with intersecting tiles of moss overlaid with a quilt of fern. Halfway through building it, I slunk away around the edge of the clearing to the far side, stepped up on a fallen oak, then plunged into a jungle of ferns, bashing my way through with a hefty club that struck and toppled them. Their emerald trowel tops bounced away and snagged around other snapped stalks, from which bled a limpid sap.

Ahead through the shadow I could see another clearing that, when I lunged through into it, was much smaller than I expected and, to my surprise, was overtaken by the rancorous carcass of a stag. I stared at it for a while as it baked in the heat and was suffused with an almost visible odour that stung my nostrils and clawed the back of my throat. Bluebottles plumed in whizzing, rising spirals out of a hidden gash beneath its hind leg as I prodded it with my hazel club. The flies regrouped into a glinting sapphire cloud, then poured down as though tipped from a jug and were sucked back into the gash, which oozed a melted red butter as the flies mined, their fizzing muffled to a ferocious hum.

I couldn't wrap my head around the fact that a stag could just die like this, in this meagre clearing, a site unfitting to its stature, as though it had crawled here out of shame or been slung here by an amateur hunter whose iffy shot had caused immeasurable discomfort.

Out of a confused desire to honour this felled king, I grabbed its biggest antler, the velveteen fuzz diaphanous in the light, and began the hard task of dragging the stag around in an arc from its cramped hideaway into the open through the passageway of crushed and buckled fern. His fur, sagged along the bowed backbone, glistened an ecru so warm I almost ran my hand through it until I saw, on closer scrutiny, the follicles were plugged with maggots. The odour, released from its shifting, was screaming. As I hauled the slumped body through the last rows of ferns, I looked back at the dollop of green-ground light that was its open-air grave. Where it had lain a depressed shadow began to prickle alive with straightening grass, the dip in shade coming level with the slightly higher, sunlit ground.

By the time I had dragged it into the main clearing, I was sweating profusely and out of breath. Others noticed what I had brought, and they rushed towards me from the surrounding browse line, abandoning their building work. Before they neared me, I let go of the antler, and the head swivelled, slackened, and thumped to the ground, its black, convex eye staring eerily into mine.

I washed my hands in a whisky-brown stream, letting it soothe through my fingers, which parted from each other in the pull of the brook. The brook bed was a mosaic of chestnut pebbles, each one reflecting the sunlight with its own particular hue, each one separated from the next by a black line no more than two millimetres wide. As I dipped each hand in the water, I distinctly felt a hollowness open up inside of me like the depressed stag-shaped patch of mossy grass I had seen in the clearing, its life framed as a heavy, fleeting trace disappearing into taut earth. Even though my hands were not stinking, I kept on washing them until they became gloved in a whiteness purer than the white of the stag's exposed bone.

A crowd of classmates loomed over the ghastly half-bare skull of the stag, sniggering and disgusted, until they were disbanded by the flustered teacher. I spent the rest of the day confined to the front seat of the school bus, nauseated by the reek of new leather, unable to eat my packed lunch.

A Good Companion

Dominic rolls out his blue sleeping bag. He lies down, reaching up around the back of his head, hooks in a bunch of ferns under the hood, creating a pillow. I nurse the fire at the shelter's entrance. The position of the stars above the heath, the situation of the full and retracted moon, tells the time as somewhere past midnight. The hatchet's bevelled head reflects the flames like a curl of mirror, and flickers.

We are not tired. He sits up, brushing his head against the fern and stick roof of our makeshift den, then crawls out to sit beside me. We face the fire. Pine cones crackle. Holly boughs seethe with moisture that bubbles and drips, fizzing into the embers. The ground is cool and damp under my palm, soft sand and dirt layered over clay – the Eocene textures that dominate the surface of the northern New Forest.

I call this place by its ancient name: Ytene. When that name was hollered, tribes had their lives here, amongst boar and eagle and wolf and gods: lives removed to a gleaming black edge where life is at its most raw, where the wild is what governs, and we defy it at our peril.

We say little, move less. The fire beckons us to be still, to speak only of what nourishes the stillness. Further off in the darkness of the forest, coming from the south, is the call of a tawny owl. A long clear ring of warbling sound spreading, widening through the September air in crystalline pulses. The call verges on the visible. My eyes, startled by my ears, search for the sound. Dominic does not live in the forest any more. He was born here, and we grew up together, like brothers, but he moved abroad when he was seventeen, to Texas, to the desert. When he comes home now and again to see his family he visits me, visits me and the forest I have never left. I think he may return for good some day. For now, we are sinking into the tree's world. I'm taking him into the place where my senses aren't merely my own but are shared by the things around me, where my awareness is of the mud as much as it is of myself. We are taken into the vast and fine aromas of a landscape I have come to cherish ever more deeply.

I spend most of my time in the forest alone, scrounging for connections with bark, bird calls, drifts of wood laid down by the woodsman for me to pick over. For long stretches, through the night and through the day, I wander, or am intensely still as a found skull, empty and aside. It is a dream of mine to become really rooted to this place, for my self to move amongst Ytene like some native species. The wind here wants me too, and the rain. I do as best I can. I notice, though, that this is all acted out in solitude, that space of acute resonance.

But what is discovered in solitude is enhanced by companionship. This is where Dominic has his place. The forest is good for us. It never ceases, from our earliest ventures to now, to bring us close. Two people tied to a land.

With him I understand what it means to share in the life of the forest, to share in the feast of relationships, human threaded through and interwoven with the inhuman. More so tonight because I have needed him. His absence has made my solitude question itself.

We plug the fire with more knife-cleaned sticks. Sparks are shaken up like a ripped and thrown flag of flame. The canopy catches them like a thousand waiting hands.

Out on the heath the heather is more still than I had guessed. The small fire at the wood's edge seems to be the only body moving. Each stalk of heather sleeps, limpid and clawed in the moonlight. I lie down and it wraps over me. I peer up through the lattice to Orion, Cassiopeia. Dominic lies down beside me. Two bodies on the heath at night, wondering, tangled in heather. The odd frog trumps. A pipistrelle flings overhead like a blown cinder, a black leaf. The honey scent of purple ling is almost blooming. Swallows and house martins and swifts will soon weave the dawn sky. The heath waits for its creatures; the forest hatches them forth.

We rise and walk west down to Black Gutter, which trickles up into a golden catchment of grasses below the ridge of Deadman's Hill. Dominic leaps over the dark stream. His feet plunge into shallow bog, releasing a tang that reeks of a carcass. He stares down at his sodden feet. Our laughter disturbs the meditation of a lone grey mare. She bolts north, her haunches quaking, her mane rippling back, covering wet ground quickly, and shouting out a thrumming whinny.

I wonder if our fire is still burning. The temptation to career back to camp is strong, but we keep heading west. The rise and fall of the land pushing us onwards in long swells of heather, water, and stars. How many times in our friendship, Dominic, have we done this, tailed off in abandonment of workaday constraints, seeking adventure? Ours is a friendship of living history that arcs forward like the strong oak boughs of the night, into the darkness of the unknown in which unseen creatures vaguely roam and the moon is a cloud undergoing a round of formation. The human effort to get into wildness sometimes requires a human counterpart along the way. Solitude without the feast of companionship is a gathering of wasted food.

The fire is still hot. We grow tired, and rest in our shelter amongst the slugs and spiders. Woken by the gruff barking of roe, rumours of daylight gather in the east. We drop plans to wait for the first hunting crow, and instead hike home so we can drive the hour to the Dorset coast and swim beneath the arch of Durdle Door, never guessing what riches are waiting for us.

The Image

Airborne,
the arcing curve of the dolphin's belly
fits around the top rim of the rising sun perfectly.
Momentarily,
the image is like a symbol
for something tremendous.
Dolphin and sun
elegantly joined in the lifting of each other
to their shared pinnacles of beauty,
a unity
from which all names fall.
As the sun pushes clear of the horizon
the dolphin slides off into the crimson sea.

Drawing Near

I had wanted to see the flamingos of Sant Carles de la Ràpita, to behold the largesse of their radiant pearl-pinks, to watch the calligraphy S of their necks unfurl as they stoop to the jade surface of the Ebro Delta. We set sail, however, as soon as we arrive at the marina. The humidity is scorching. Cross-hatched clouds of mosquitoes sway up from murky emerald lagoons, and move like smoke across the water.

Amy is excited not so much about where we are but about the prospect of sailing with her father, with whom she hasn't sailed since she was a child. They hold hands as they walk down the pontoon, talking and laughing about their memories of sailing together, about the trip ahead. Their two uneven shadows roll out behind them. It has been too long since they spent time in such devotion to one another's presence. Fearing that I may be an encroachment upon their reparation, I linger behind, hoping this trip will bring them to a common solace.

As we kick off from the pontoon, slacken and unleash ropes, and slide the boat out of the marina, one heron casually lifts from a tidal barrier of rocks. Grunting twice, it almost flies above the mast, crossing between us and the belligerent sun, its shadow briefly one of the crew. The heron beats diligently and earnestly north towards the Ebro lagoon to unobtrusively take its place, I imagine, at the edge of a thousand busy flamingos. I point out the heron to Amy; she smiles. Her father is at the steering wheel, his nautical cap pulled on tightly over thin drapes of silver hair. He is happy to be under way. A warm wind skitters through the snapping sail.

Around midnight, after eight hours of continuous sailing from the eastern mainland of Spain, we reach Islas Columbretes. From his position as skipper behind the steering wheel, my father-in-law tells me the main island, Illa Grossa, was once part of an enormous volcano. That is all he knows about our night's point of rest. I am finding out where we are going as we go, restlessly walking around the boat in mild agitation. Amy alternates between lying down on the cushioned bench in quiet contemplation and sitting beside her father. She notes how his pale skin has already started to freckle into a tan, and compares her arm to his, their forearms touching to form a single limb of separate ages.

Emerging from the sea and sky, the full span of Illa Grossa looms into view like an affront. A distinct remnant of an ancient crater, composed of basalt. Over a kilometre in length and rising to 67 metres at its highest point, the island is isolated and imposing. Overtaken by an uneasy wonder, we warily sail by, cowering in the broad and smooth-backed hills of swell that roll beneath us from the north, and buck away soundlessly to the south.

After hoisting down the mainsail, packing it snugly into its long hammock suspended over the boom, kneading it neatly inside with my fists like working dough into rolls, fastening salt-crusted ties in oversized loops around its girth to secure it in place, I hold the mainmast, stretch out, and survey the island. At this hour, its vast silhouette is hardly distinguishable from the Mediterranean night, a piece of land not quite cut free from its place of creation. Stars above look like flung spots of lava frozen in time, beguiling in their stasis.

There are no visible structures of human endeavour except for the automatic lighthouse. At the furthest headland, it swings its wide and shuddering beam across the sheen of black sea, illuminating the whites of the breaking waves into incandescent lines of exploding quartz, riding up the vertically curving walls of basalt escarpments, then shining out beyond to the stars. The place is left alone. I wonder what creatures have Illa Grossa as their home? Colonies of stray life, human or not, perhaps a forgotten species of falcon. My mind runs away with the fantasy of where we are.

My father-in-law, at the tiller wheel, lets the boat drift further into the island's half-amphitheatre until the cliffs surround and extend beyond us on both sides, harbouring a confining stillness and a confiding silence in its wild enclosure. Our entry here feels more like a trespass than a visit, an obvious incision into a place that takes care of itself. We listen in on signs of life, inklings.

A novice to sailing, to the obstacle-laden terrain of a yacht, I stumble over a hopscotch of ropes, levers, and cleats, in order to reach the forward pulpit. It is my role to release the anchor. I am nervous that I might get it wrong. Turning a small chrome bar shaped like a T, I lift a heavy door and strap it with bungee cords around the wire railings that run the length of the boat on either side like allotment fences. I am aware that it's important to drop the anchor before the boat drifts too far in or turns askew into the swell. Heaving out the anchor head that's shaped like an elongated anvil and which shines intermittently silver in the beam of the lighthouse, the chrome coming at me in flashes, I yank and slide out a crossbar, then let the anchor head jolt over the furthest point of the bow, over the elbow of the gunwale. It pauses over the sea. Looking back to my father-in-law, who signals release with a thumbs up, I press a red button on a remote control that's attached to the inside wall of the anchor hold. Leaning out like the boat's figurehead, I watch carefully as the anchor head drops, smoothly followed by the chain, which uncoils from the twisted mass heaped down in the hold and raps the front angle of the bow as it descends. A clattering of echoes emit across the obsidian horseshoe of the island, like the furious strikes of a blacksmith's hammer. Amy comes to stand beside me, to watch the anchor and to share her expertise.

At the Gatling-gun strikes of the chain, gull-like wails retaliate, strained shrieks cannonading across the inner cliffs. We both look up, alert and wide-eyed. Absorbed, however, in dropping the anchor correctly, I only half hear the boisterous and piercing cacophony. The anchor head continues to drop into the water. Reels of chain rattle out, coil after coil. After twenty metres – indicated by a strip of red tape – I release the automatic switch and the chain clunks tight, wobbling in restricted circles as the anchor head digs itself into the seabed. The boat slides away from the anchor, hauling the chain away from the bow like a guy rope.

Pleased with the boat's placement, my father-in-law steps away from the wheel and sits on one of two benches built into either side of the companionway, leaning over his knees, holding the bench either side of his hips. He finds a lantern and hangs it on the bar above us. Amy hands him his jumper; she pulls a black shawl around her own shoulders. We step down through the hatch into the hot cabin to make a meal of fruit, bread, and cheese. They cut the bread together more steadily than I can in the lolling cabin.

The unusual sounds become more apparent during the quiet after our food, a quiet of fatigue precipitated by a long day of travel through unchanging scenes: an omnipresence of blue sea laid out beneath an omnipotent sun. We say little in the glow of the lantern, in the harsher and additional glow of the passing beam of the lighthouse that picks out the bronze highlights in Amy's dusky hair, and casts her father's grey with dashes of golden ash.

I have never heard animal calls like this before. Amy and I try to guess what creatures they might be. My father-in-law wants to participate but is too tired and goes down into the cabin to sleep. Sitting on opposite sides of the companionway, Amy and I face each other, listening out for the calls that have filled the inner curve of Illa Grossa, a curve like an ear, with a nocturnal orchestra of otherworldly instruments. Unable to match calls to creatures, our eyes blinded by the solid darkness of the surroundings, we give up on our guessing game. The lateness of the hour is palpable. Amy steps down into the cabin. I stay up on deck, enthralled by the babbling of voices yelling in broken unison like an audience in the stadium of the island cheering themselves into vociferous riot. Calls replete with a kind of panic, fractured and disparate; calls in the key of quick-fire ratcheting, contortions, voices fitting to Illa Grossa. Peering down through the hatch, I see Amy and her father are sleeping on built-in beds situated either side of the cabin, facing each other. Their hands, tucked beneath the single pillows, mirror one another. I see their likeness, both lying there like seeds. What it takes to bring kin close.

As I lie there the sounds are too strange for me to sleep. If only I knew what animals these were, could put a picture in my mind to their calls, to gain a sense of completeness. Like a lit fuse running rapidly and crackling in crescendo from one end of Illa Grossa to the other, the crying does not relent, and builds perpetually towards a concluding outburst.

Our arrival here has sparked their anxious performance, is an interruption of their peace. Watching the V beam of light slide up and over the cliffs, I look for signs, glints, reflections, and movements of the rowdy secrecy of animals, until I am overpowered by fatigue. The boat rocks in the motion of the swell and their uproar, their maimed choir, is the last sound I hear before I pull a blanket over me and give in to sleep's motion. Directly above me, the mast's top dot of light, revolving and swinging like a broken timepiece, is a star to the black crescent moon of the island. The bright beam of the lighthouse swoops over my closed eyes like a fluorescent wing.

I awake facing the sea running past and behind, slick and burnished with phosphorescent oils of molten copper, indigo, and more colours of subdued and lustrous magnificence. No wind, no swell, only the faint tumbling slosh of water around the bow, along the grey and blue fibre-glass hull, the engine purring at six knots as we slice our way eastward towards Ibiza. Illa Grossa is out of sight, gone in the seam of haze between sea and sky. I never saw it in the daylight, that island. An enigma of dark land colonised by unnamed creatures, full of beckoning. I fear that I might forget those calls.

My father-in-law rests, dozes, his cap pulled over his eyes for shade. His daughter is still sleeping down in the cabin. I take the wheel and watch the sun rise sharp as an axe blade, cleaving definition into the horizon with a light that is not too brutal to stare at. All around the boat, the glycerine-blue of the sea begins to show through the swathes of orange-amber and yellow-umber, like stained water filtered clear through a silk cloth dyed with a rich, tawny glow. Those colours dissolve as the burning globe of the sun lifts into the sky; a triumphant ignition. I keep looking back past the transom, which, as the yacht slides east, leaves a wake like a disappearing road to Illa Grossa. By gazing towards the place we've left behind, I have let the boat veer off course by a few degrees, the course illuminated by the Raymarine chartplotter. I swing it back round, and set it on autopilot. The island has a hold on me, the riveting uncertainty of that dark place spins weirdly in my mind, like a dream cut short too soon.

By mid-morning, the triangular flaps pulled down from the packaged sail either side of the companionway giving us shade from the sun, Amy reading her book, my father-in-law standing beside me, we are over halfway to the western coast of Ibiza.

Our talk alternates between the immediate scenes and Amy's reminiscences of her first journeys with her father on their family boat, *Alpha*, interspersed with long periods of silence. Nothing is strained. There is none of the tension Amy feared would arise between herself and her father. I feel her relief. Talk comes and goes and we are relaxed into one another, relaxed into where we are. I do not feel excluded from their family ties, their stories. I listen to them as I listen to the breeze cracking like a whip in the shade-flaps and to the water lightly crashing across the hull in tossed bucketloads. Amy takes the big wheel as her father stands beside her pointing out almost invisible objects on the horizon. Their eyes settle on the blue. The horizon brings them close, the zenith tilts back their shoulders. Eyes of a father and eyes of a daughter filled with expectancy, with the richness of the distance ahead. Shared view stemming from shared blood.

With Amy's encouragement, I sit at the forward pulpit, at the very head of the boat. My legs dangle over the side, almost touching spray as the bow rises and falls to the boat's gentle acceleration, carving its way through soothing water. My back is upright against the mast. I look back now and again at Amy, who smiles at me, knowing how much I am relishing sitting here, nothing between myself and the horizon but sea.

Flushed with exhilaration and a kind of fierce tranquillity, I understand why Amy and her father adore sailing, why it is the one venture that most brings them together into total acceptance of one another, how the spaciousness of sea and sky can accommodate their differences and nurture their similarities, bringing an aspect of their life together that will always be cherished through the vicissitudes of time. I look back down the boat and see a father and daughter who are no longer estranged. A nexus of trust takes shape, moods of healing. I have never witnessed them so at ease with one another.

Mainland Ibiza has yet to show an edge, a ragged fragment of itself. Off to the front starboard side, at about ninety metres, I spot a spume that I take for a freak wave amongst this flat expanse. Jolted out of my reverie, I jump to my feet. The splash appears again, a definite interruption, a crease in the calm. A fin pokes through the surface, a wedge of tenebrous sapphire, wet and glinting. Then it submerges, gone for a taut minute, until the fin pierces the surface, this time less than twenty metres from the bow and closing, closing with unrelenting intention. Shark? Apparition? The fin bolts down and comes up on the boat's port side. The whole animal is in splendorous view through the transparent water. Dolphin.

I shout, 'Dolphin, dolphin,' pointing emphatically at the gorgeous animal glimmering beneath the surface that flickers over it, constantly revealing the shine of the animal's strength and elegance as it jives to and fro, coming in close to the bow, hiding in the fountains of white water erupted by the bow ploughing onwards, then swinging back out into the blue. Amy rushes to the bow, stands breathless, staring with me. My father-in-law leaves the boat to steer itself, hops up to the main deck from the tiller, and joins us in a rush of enthusiasm. Each one of us is gawking and rapt, craning forward over the wire railing to get a closer view of the stunning, lithe animal, the utter perfection of its profile as it skims silently through the water, winning against the bow in speed, dropping back again to pick up the chase, breaking, now and again, with bellow-like exhumations of air, its body tilted away to fix its shining dark eye onto mine, onto ours. All three of us like children, a rapt group, in awe, stand locked and liberated into a surcharged exchange of eyes, nerves, flesh, with an extreme centre of intelligence, the dolphin.

My father-in-law briskly walks back to the wheel, to steer the boat right. Amy stays with me, stays with the animal. We study it ecstatically. It is so beautiful as to be harrowing. Then, in a scintillation of flipper, belly, fin, the dolphin almost leaps out of the water entirely, but, teasing us, then merges into the deeper level of blue, and vanishes. The trace of its voltage prickles through the salt-swept air.

Back in the companionway Amy and her father begin to talk animatedly about the times they saw dolphins leaping after *Alpha* in the Aegean Sea, fifteen years ago. The dolphin resonates through them, memories of dolphins and now, the now that will become a memory in time, gathering them to each other in a shared and living history. They are brought near to one another by the dolphin into the intense affinity of the shared life.

The frank shock of the dolphin evoked in each one of us, the ways we were so interested in the glimpse of its life, proved that not only as individuals but as a group, a family, we had room to respond to the unpredictable, to be taken in by a simple and bare encounter with a wild animal, totemic in its power. It threw open our hearts, and something binding and wonderful blew in. The wild dolphin made us a speechless congregation.

With Ibiza not yet in view, we settle down again to placid routines of reading, sleeping, talking, watching, and silence. We look out for more dolphins, our nerves still tingling in the aftermath of its blistering raid on our senses. We stay in that open space for as long as we can, renewing a confidence within us that we are still capable, as when we were children, of being bowled over by an animal, even an animal for which we have a name.

The dark incompleteness of Illa Grossa, its caterwauling creatures, the glimmering dolphin performing hide-and-seek in the marvellous blue, my wife, a daughter, and her father, our very selves – the unfathomable mysteries of these relationships are hopeful antidotes against fixations to hoard a place, a person, an animal, in its entirety. We lose what we hoard, and the door closes once again.

Water dashes against the hull. The engine rumbles. Ibiza heaves into view. Sky and sea merge to fling us through this world, a world that beckons, beckons, to be admired, loved, as it passes.

The Ewe

Poplars were very still at the track's edge, their leaves pronouncing the deadening heat of the noon sun. The white sides of those leaves shone like shards of glass; their green sides seemed to melt like dye running off hands. Plodding up from Filoti, a village in the central mountains of Naxos, Greece, Amy and I slowly made our way around the southern base of Mount Zeus, the tallest mountain on the island. The hyperactivity of the cicadas in the poplars was oppressive, increasing our drowsiness.

Cedar trees, tough and gnarled, formed a scant barrier at the precipitous bend in the track as it swung out, away from the mountain, and dangled us over a parched valley. Cypress trees, bush, the odd poplar, were the most abundant vegetation and, save for the poplar, dotted the surfaces of other mountains. Great rocks astounded me. I found myself pausing in the crushing heat either to stare at some lone boulder on the shoulder of a distant hill or to run my hand over a rock at the track's edge, feeling the grain and warmth. Two buzzards circled the sun like the hands of a clock lifting itself away into a resplendent sky. Copper bells rattled and tinkled in the valleys; far away, the guttural bleating of goats echoed, their sounds adding volume to the landscape. Through a gap between two mountains towards the south, the Aegean Sea was not visible in itself, only the sun on another world of twilight blue, deep and broad. Facing east from the track, emery mountains petered out to a wide plain that blended seamlessly into the blue world beyond, the very colour of the border that runs between the known and the unknown; here where the sun frazzles the skin, hammers the eye, and out there, where minds that make myths have their abodes in undisturbed serenity.

At Aria Spring we rested in the shade of a tall cedar. Limpid water bubbled out from a wrist-wide cleft in a rock and pooled in a shallow well harassed by a swarm of lemon-yellow hornets. Clinging on to the slightly cooler air above the water, the hornets formed a barricade around the well. Now and again, one would fling itself out and zip over our heads, fly manically around the cedar, then rejoin the swarm that mirrored, in a group dance, the undulations of the pool as the spring pulsed into it.

On the other side of the spring, encircled by a low brick wall, was the largest olive tree I had seen in Naxos. Perhaps the wall signalled its uniqueness. Giving the hornets a wide berth, I walked out of the shade and into the stark, bright heat in which the olive tree grew, its trunk wrinkled and gnarled, with a texture like bristled leather. As I walked slowly around the tree on the low brick wall, I came across a ewe. She was lying on her side, her back firmly against the tree, out of the shade and in the fullness of the sun. Her eyes, lined with whisker-like eyelashes, were half closed. She was too weak to react to my presence. Amy rushed over, and we both bent down low beside her. Her stomach was bulging and taut, showing signs of pregnancy. A black and red viscous liquid, like lava cooling, puddled around her back end. Flies mobbed her. Her breathing was rapid. Marooned there, far from the flocks that could be heard but not seen down in the valley, we wondered where the shepherd was, why this ewe had, obviously, been here for such an agonising length of time. She winced with every breath, no more than a fading farrago, two bodies in one, the weight of the unborn draining her own life from her.

I scrambled down a thistle-crowded ledge and jumped onto a lower but less used path at the head of which stood a leaning house. I looked through cracks in the sun-bleached wood into the dark interior, but no one stirred. Over crisp leaves I jogged further down the path until it brought me to a dilapidated cabin. Bags of herd feed were stored under the porch. A lone hen clucked in a cramped cage, scraping the hard sandy ground with a mangled foot. Propped up against the front door was a shepherd's crook. Chained to a steel post was a mongrel dog that, only when it saw me, growled and pawed forwards until the chain snapped tight and he couldn't move. There was a TV on the floor inside, a ripped couch draped with clothes, and a pan of potatoes. One window. Powdery dust rose and fell in the light. But no one. The ewe and the home were abandoned.

When I got back to Amy and the ewe, my shins cut by the thistles, the ewe's breathing was beating as slowly as a heart in a sleeping body, and her heart was weaker than her breathing. Amy cupped water in her hands from the spring and brought it close to the ewe's grey and crackled lips. It did not entice her. The water splashed upon the ground, a vanishing blot.

She died in the dust, in the fallen olive leaves, the interior light gone out, the exterior light blazing and unforgiving. Where was the protector of the herds? We did not ascend Mount Zeus that day.

The Wonder

Have the stars lost their mind,
swaying in their collapsed constellations?
Fireflies are drawn westward into the dark,
over the boar's up-tilted tusk,
through ruins of a stone barn,
swirling, stopping
where my wonder wakes
and walks out to hold them.

Fireflies of Podere Conti

The relative coolness of the veranda's white porcelain tiles against my back as I lay there was fragile relief from the imposing and unrelenting strength of the night's heat. The airless room of the old farmhouse made me too breathless to sleep. Somehow Amy managed to snooze, harassed by mosquitoes, sweat beading from her brow, lit by an edge of moonlight that was coming in from mountains above the dark forest. I rolled onto my right side, propping up my head with my right arm. I watched an amber spider with darker amber legs make its way lazily along the edge of the veranda, then crawl off onto the hard and almost grassless ground that extended away in a gradual incline towards the stars, towards familiar constellations.

We had arrived there after a whole day driving south from Lake Garda, leaving a breezy shoreline of waves kissing stones and distended green figs hanging and nodding from fig trees, their roots spread out through the clear shallows. The temperatures crept higher and higher to a peak of bewildering intensity by the time we reached Pontremoli, taking a narrow track that snaked up into the mountains of the Tuscan border, coming to rest at a remote farmhouse named Podere Conti. A limping golden retriever with a scab-ridden neck met us with an enthusiastic welcome. He rolled onto his back, his long pink tongue trembling out from the side of his panting mouth. Our own two dogs, Daisy and Dilly, Welsh collies of cooler climes, immediately sought out shade beneath the timber roof of the porch. We swam in the pool and drank water and ate fruit until the sun set behind the beech woods crackling loudly with a vast population of ratcheting cicadas. Bees wearily ghosted the spent taupes and dull purples of sun-shrivelled lavender. Fat hornets glided back and forth in straight lines. From the shade of our veranda I watched them making determined journeys from one edge of the dry and furrowed field to the other, losing them occasionally in the hazy crimson light of the setting sun that, somewhere further off, was throwing light upon the green mountains. Down here, surrounded by the dense beech and oak woods, the darkness of evening began, bringing with it another kind of heat, less raw but no less harsh than the day's. Our dogs hardly stirred.

We would leave the next day for a cooler place. Our whole trip was meant to be one of our last adventures alone together before the birth of our child, time before that beautiful interruption. No planning, only a vague idea that we wanted to head south from our home in the New Forest, drive through the Alps and down into Italy, then loop back up and around, along the Atlantic coast of France.

Past midnight, I lay on the veranda with Daisy and Dilly, hearing the crunch of branches in the dark distance that I took for a wild boar, then I went out for a night walk. The half-moon was enough light to guide my way out on the hard and pocked earth of the field, over a stone bridge arcing gently across a dry riverbed, round stones glinting in the moonlight, the undefined shadows of beech leaves patterned along the visible stretch of the riverbed. I leaned over the edge of the bridge, hearing again the crash of sticks and scrape of leaves in the distance, the boar running, my dogs either side of me, their ears stretched out and high, alert. I imagined the water that must flow down there, flushing over the stones in moonlight, the coolness of it rising in layers to meet my downturned eyes.

Daisy and Dilly bounded ahead into the darkness of the wood, taking a deeply rutted path that climbed, eventually, above the treeline. Other paths led away left and right into the woods. I stopped and stared, trying to make out the shapes of the trees, the denser darkness between them, the mystery beyond. I looked back at the moonlit, forested hills rolling away in all directions, such a wild and undisturbed region of land in the silence of the night. Except for the single light from the farmhouse down in the valley, there were no other visible constructions. I thought of the deer and boar hunters using the paths down there in the wood, creeping over the hills, knowing the terrain like the body knows its bones.

Proceeding further up, I broke my way through an entanglement of thicket, coming right up against a stone wall and a rough oval space large enough for me to duck through. I stepped into a ruined barn or home – I could not tell, it was so dark. The dogs, on the other hand, did not follow but waited outside. The ceiling was lofty, in parts caved in, leaving openings to the stars, allowing in the glow of faraway moonlight. Placing my hand upon the flaking and crumbling stone of the buckled walls, I couldn't help but think of what had gone on here, the people who might have made their lives here in these woods, these hills. A narrow corridor led away from the bigger room, drifting into total darkness. I peeked around the corner, testing the safety of the timber floor with a hesitant heel. The hollow, rattling thud of the timbers indicated rot but I was careless enough to step forward into the total dark onto timbers that, for all I knew, precariously hid a void below. Bringing my eyes up slowly from my almost invisible feet, I spotted what I thought was a cluster of flickering stars through an opening in the wall. Peering closer, too afraid to cross the room itself over the weak and rotten timbers, I saw a delicate swarm of fireflies. Twenty or so, silent and each one a light unto itself and to the glowing swarm, jinked, rose, and dropped, purling a pattern of enthralling chaos. They enticed my attention to the point that all I saw was fireflies, not even the darkness between or surrounding them or the ruin itself and the imposing stones; all I saw was a random murmuration of light, a shattered globe still attached by invisible threads, growing and fading in size, beating like a heart, consuming me in their dance. I wanted to put my hand amongst them but the loose timbers rattled and rocked when I took a mere half-step forward.

Their bioluminescence sang. How can a life form so small elicit a human response, a feeling that lies dormant in our run-of-the-mill lives, shakes us out from habitual ways of experience? Wonder is a vicious opening of the primal airway between oneself and the world, a radical clearing of that essential connection. I could breathe again.

I cannot recall how long I remained in that ruin staring into the dance of the fireflies, utterly enamoured with their bodies of light drawing and undrawing shapes in the dark like magnesium-lit sparklers whirring through the air, spelling words too fast to shape with a dumbstruck mouth. But they did disperse, away into the furthest corners of the dark room, perhaps flowing out one by one towards the stars above the hills. My own consciousness returned to me like a heavy stone to bear back down into the excruciating heat of the farmhouse in the valley.

The Orangutan

She slides her hands through steel bars
complicit as a veteran criminal to a repeated arrest,
on show to my tender gawking.

I inspect the lines that criss-cross cut
her dark and bark-ancient palms,
hands shaped to the heft of fruit and branch.

Heart lines, lines of longevity,
lines of lives before this,
suggestions of more freedom before
the storm of man.

The story of this orangutan's life
is far more than what human eyes surmise.
In essence, she cannot be contained
even though she sits here upon cobbled concrete
behind bars,
looking at me with expanding eyes nested in a shock of
    orange hair,
the way she would if she saw the fires blazing through
    her home,
the sound of a thousand chainsaws roaring,
the bulldozers and the men,
the forest smoking with silence.

I am the destroyer,
the maniac thrashing in his human cage.

A Full Moon in Borneo

Whilst the gibbon's yawp ricocheted in widening, echoless rings throughout the surrounding jungle, my eyes were drawn to the moonlit web of a stationary spider. The web was threaded from the lower end of the stair railing all the way to the far lower corner of the hut. I ducked below the web's translucent canvas and looked up through it at the moon so high and pinched, misty and undefined, in a spare space of night sky. Tremulous to my breath, the web acted like a lens to the moon and its light poured down into the upper levels of the canopy, made up of clawing trees whose names I did not know. The gibbon yawped again.

I remained beneath the web's shattered and stretched umbrella until I saw a spider, black and rounded, still as a stone, at about three o'clock on the web's elongated clock face. I inched to the right and knelt cautiously and directly below the gem-like sheen of the plump spider, its thin legs slightly kinked up in readiness or rest. The spider looked as though it was on the moon because the moon was behind it, and the web was like the moon's spider-shaped shadow. I was called into the hut, away from my reveries, by our guide as supper was ready. I also needed to remove the leeches that somehow had latched on to my kneecaps, through my khaki trousers.

I was going to miss the jungle. The adventure. But more than that, I think, I was going to miss Doris. The adolescent female orangutan I had become attached to over the four weeks of volunteering at the rehabilitation centre where she resided. This was the final night in Borneo, spent on an overnight trek through some of the last patches of primary rainforest in that area, looking out for orangutans, finding nests that sat like tree houses high up in the dense canopy. I knew, of course, that my attachment to Doris, my close interactions and tender observations of her, had developed in a fabricated environment, in a centre, surrounded by unnatural things, and would, therefore, never occur out there in the wilder parts where the orangutans ghost through the trees and our human presence is studied from afar, glared at through rustling canopies as they brachiate onwards, deeper into the forest, searching for a mate, for food, for the right site to make their big nests for the night.

Outside the hut a stream gurgled, something crashed through the branches, distant creatures yelped and bleeped and called. The night jungle was an orchestra of mysterious yells. Lying on the camp bed beneath the cone of the mosquito net, I listened to the voices of the forest, knowing that not too far away the slayers of the trees, the palm-oil tycoons, were approaching, slashing and burning away the forest with relentless intensity. How long would it take before they reached here, this hut, this stream? I thought of Doris back in the centre, a day's walk away, sleeping in the hammock of old ropes in the cage, waiting to be released one day, waiting. By the time she would be ready the forest might be in cinders, a cemetery. I drifted in and out of sleep, recollecting every moment with her. Her quick and steady look, the way her eyes invaded me, the texture of her hair as she turned away and pressed her back up against the bars, curls of coarse orange hair poking through, inspected and rolled between my finger and thumb. I had grown attached to her, drawn into a relationship that I will never forget, but I will always remain aware that such a relationship shouldn't have been the case. She should have been swinging through the trees.

Another Astronomy

Smoke from garden fires
clouds the stars above the house.

Does home now become an instant constellation
or a preparation to be made so?
From town, Brother, we have walked
an avenue of observatories
to the final one before the sea.

The father rummaging to fix a fuse,
a mother's voice is a night light in a blackout.
Then there are those breathings prior
to what we deem as ours.

We linger in the flicker of porch light
on the dew-decked lawn
among glistening beads of reflected fires
that burst in nervous hands
as we kneel to make stars of the ground
trying to mimic how Grandma would sew.

Nightly you tell me the science
of how bricks can bruise inward at dusk
then you drink the water from the bedside table
so I go thirsty through my dreams.

The Hollow of Shell Bay

I wake before you. No full morning light fills the room. Darkness begins thinning to ochre grey with the advent of dawn. One moth, the colour of rain-washed wheat, trembles and clicks against the skylight above our bed, which, in this corner of the house, sits beneath outreaching oak branches that brush the roof tiles with their wind-stirred summer leaves. Somewhere in the garden a blackbird sings.

You are lying on your right side, facing me. I am on my left side, facing you. Your stillness is beguiling. The freckles littered across your skin are like a flock of chestnut-coloured stars. I should name their constellations, become an astronomer of your skin. Your faint summer tan lends an earthen depth. The richness and tone of your dusky henna hair is as hauntingly captivating as the woods that border our home. I study the creation that you are before you are disturbed and begin to stir.

Your breathing is deep, slow, and meditative. I match my breathing to yours. The white duvet is folded over your half-revealed shoulders in a way that suggests you have not shifted an inch all night. I look at your closed eyes, the eyelids encompassing the darkness through which lit images of dreams flicker in and out. Regardless of how many times I have run my eyes like this over the contours of your familiar, sleeping face, I arrive at the knowledge that who you are and what moves you to be *you* remains unfathomable. There is a mystery as definite as your features that holds my gaze. It is a gift to lie like this beside a loved one.

The room is now plush grey, thickening to the first ashen golds of morning. The resistance of your body encased in sleep seems an act of defiance against the incremental motions of the approaching day. Though it is time to rise I do not want to wake you. I fear what the day may bring the moment your waiting illness pounces.

Yesterday it dogged you, put you out on a lonely plain of barren lifelessness, ruined the plans you had made to garden, to swim, and to see friends. It took all your energy and gave none of it back. Your eyes burned from all the tears until, in the evening, you slipped into sleep's balm.

The professionals call it bipolar II. Whatever it is, it is a part of your sense of the world. Sometimes you say it is a dark cloud enveloping you into its cell, sometimes you say it's a dark hand that holds you back from the joys you know in your heart. It is a wracking sorrow for something lost you cannot name, a gut-wrenching grief for a life not permitted to be yours. If only you saw yourself as I see you this morning you would be found, healed. There are no visible signs of it anywhere on you this morning. That is its guile; it undoes you from within.

You begin to wake. Your eyelids flutter like the first testing, hesitant wings of fledgling birds. The innocence of your eyes opening onto me before they know what they are seeing is as wondrous as the dawn light that now flows in through the curtains. As you sit up, I place a third pillow behind you. We say good morning, smile. I bring you tea, a bowl of muesli. You seem good today. Your eyes are sore from yesterday's crying, underlined with crescents of blistering shadow. But you hate to be nursed, to be thought of as a patient.

We decide to go to Shell Bay, one of our favourite places. Strong south-west winds are forecast and we are excited at the prospect of big waves. Shell Bay offers you a taste of unstained happiness, of an ordinary day without agony, and we put our trust in its remedial vigour. Your mournful flatness seems a distant thing there, a pain uncovered, flushed from its hiding into the huge blue sky against which it seems small, inconsequential.

At times I cannot wholly carry your affliction, because I do not know where to stand in relation to it, what to say, or what to do. It is hard at times not to perceive it as a demon. But when we go to Shell Bay, we find each other again. This place, like the care of a parent, lifts the weight of your burden.

We leave at noon under the intense glare of the sun. The wind is gale force, buffeting our car sideways as we rumble off the chain ferry. On either side of the timber boardwalk that leads us from the car park to the first sands, a profusion of pale umber seethes in capricious gusts of wind. Two mallards tip from side to side in their flight, and are chased into the distance. Glimpsed through crowds of gnarled sessile oak is the sea boiling and churning, a volcano of deep blues, emeralds, and whites. The wind hits us, louder than the waves that crash on the shore. We turn our backs to it, watching the sand whipping from the dunes in long, ghostly laces. Washed by wind and sand and sun, we are giddy.

We turn and stand hand in hand, hunkered into the full force of the gale, amidst ceaseless sand tearing down the length of Shell Bay. The black hood of your jacket, billowing out from around your head, hides half your face from me. When I try to look at you, sand flicks into the corners of my eyes like fine, sharp hail. I keep my head down, and push my left hand out blindly. I am searching for a passage through the wind and sand towards an imagined calm. Wide belts of dull gold sand, slightly lifted from the darker, wetter layer of stable sand beneath, whip, lacerate, burst, and rush. A black-backed gull is hurled helplessly overhead; three oystercatchers passively follow. It seems as though the whole world is tearing past us in some ultimate turn of desolation.

Tiring, our hands loosen from one another and we drift apart – I towards the shoreline, you towards the dunes. Waves rise and pound the beach. Strands of seaweed glisten, razor shells roll away like lost letters. A lone cormorant, dark and agile as an arrow, a hundred metres or so out from where I stand, attempts to fly into the wind but is beaten up and down and back around over the grabbing waves. As I turn to see where you are, sand spits into my mouth and my teeth crunch as on salted glass. Beneath the high dunes you are a black dot, unmoving as a rock. I make my way across the bay, leaning into the robust current of the sand-flecked wind, and I slump down beside you.

We are slightly protected by the dunes and by the stout clumps of marram grass that rattle like shaken maracas. Facing each other, we bring our hoods together to form a small canopy, a pocket of silence and shelter. In the shared quiet and blissful intimacy beneath our hoods, I feel as though we are seeing out the end of the world together. I bring my hands into yours against the radiating warmth of your cheek. This must have been the spot of calm I had been pushing towards. Not to talk about pain, your pain, but to be silent before each other, filled with love, in the refuge of Shell Bay. Your hopelessness and my failed attempts to heal trail away from us in the wind, into the distance. Nothing else defines you or us except the completeness of this moment, in which there is no sorrow, only the joyous fusion of our hearts, beating in the wind like seabirds rising free.

We decide to climb up the dunes, to sit amongst the grasses. You find a space between two knolls, and encourage me to go swimming, knowing it is what I need most. The wind hammers my bare body, but the sun is warm enough to ease my run from the dunes to the sea through the crossfire of sand. I do not realise how much I have needed this liberation until I dive through the wall of the first wave and explode out the other side, gasping for the breath robbed by the cold of the water. Swimming against the force of the current is useless so I give in, let go. The waves buoy me, lifting me up as though I were a child, and effortlessly carry me back to the shore. I turn and go back into the water, wanting more.

You wave from the dunes through the thick haze of sun and wind-blown sand like a shimmering mirage. I return the gesture but I don't think you can see me hidden in the deep troughs between the waves. My heart beats fast in a panic of elation. You were right. I needed this, this wildness, to feel strong again, prepared, renewed. I let go, go limp in the sea and the waves ferry me on their shoulders as I fall and tumble into the white wash that roars around my submerged head. I clamber out of the sea on the ride of a tumbling wave, and run towards you. You wrap a towel around me. I cannot stop smiling, laughing.

The wind comes at us from a new angle, riding up the face of the dune, throwing up plumes of sand that shower down upon us in rasps. We seek refuge further into the dunes. I take a last look back at the sea, at its storm of electric blues.

Following a maze of narrow paths through heather, out of sight of the sea and the bay, but still in the brunt of the wind, we wander — at times you lead me and then I lead you — seeking shelter. Deep in the heather where the paths peter out, we come upon a grassy slope that gently extends three metres or so into a hollow of vivid short green grass, smooth as a lawn.

Holding hands, we descend into the hollow, a bowl shaped like two hands cupped together for the humble and grateful receiving of a gift. A crater of peace, balmy and brimming with sunlight, entirely out of the wind, a secret pocket of silence in the surface of the earth. We feel blessed to have found this place. It is a cradle. I sit up with my back against the side of the hollow, your head in my lap, the length of your body supine under the sun and blue sky. Your eyes close, naturally. I run my fingers over your face. It seems that we have found the most peaceful place on earth. No cold shadows of sorrow. Your illness cannot find us. I run my fingers through the warmth of your hair. We do not bother ourselves with what tomorrow may bring or what yesterday brought. There is only this present moment of a cherishing green light.

Above us the wind flows through the heather, and beyond the waves rise and fall, rise and fall, each bursting with its own shine as it hisses to extinction upon the shore. I hold you tightly, not wanting to leave. I watch you sleeping once again.

Autumn

Feral

Scrumping friends – these lithe limbs
our crop was got by, a slick show –
terra firma meant surprise.
Where do we land from our heights now?

Between a spiked crown of branches
was our trapdoor,
our high way earthward. You first, then I
freewheeling down into an asylum of dung,

proud and fragrant with apple rot,
rabid with child joy and stolen stash,
hailing down the sun to share in our elemental feast.

Father

Becs de Bosson, 3,149 metres

Dad, in his olive-green and indigo checked nightshirt, leans out of the top window of the Cabane des Becs de Bosson, a two-storey mountain hut perched in a lone position upon the edge of a wide and undulate col, 2,980 metres above sea level, in the Pennine Alps of southern Switzerland. I am standing outside, wrapped in my down jacket. We are both looking eastward, waiting for sunrise.

There is a rising sharpness to the dark that, as it dispels, carves out near and far things into gradually stunning relief. Flowers, some with names I know and some of which I am ignorant, sparsely surround my boots as they hug the ground. I bend and rub the petal of a flower between finger and thumb, its form barely visible in the half-dark, contained in a sleep of indolent purple. The flowers dream of their fulfilment in the forthcoming sun. There is no wind as such, only cool eddies of air that roll and spiral in small acrobatics, then become still and vanish. Scattered embryonic wind.

Dad and I are part of and witness to what is taking shape before the show of light. Colours, textures, are slowly becoming manifest under a governance of motion that ushers and compels, withdrawing once those colours and textures begin to take hold of themselves. But it is still hazy with the waning darkness. Dad has never been so hushed. The land places a finger across its lips. We listen.

The Pas de Lona is a sunken, hidden plateau encircled by toothed ridges of shadow-bone schist and gneiss of midnight greys and sparkling blacks, of snowless peaks that rise up like ruins of an ancient civilisation, then ebb away to a line of higher, snow-clad mountains. A culmination of secrets is shared amongst the lives of this place to which we are granted access. I am grateful.

Further ahead from where I am, to the left and right in a broken, statuesque line, stand the five others in our group. Each one of us is separated by a space shaped by the desire for solitude. It is right, this grouping of people. To huddle and crowd and talk would be unnatural to the moment, insensitive. We need room for what is happening, to take root in it. In some unconscious way we are stepping into the lead of the land, willing to grow into the day moulding into itself.

As I look up to my immediate left at Dad in the window, his forearms crossed beneath his chest, his head up, leaning forward, he points commandingly to the east. The first light. A narrow funnel of pale crimson floats down through two adjacent snowy mountains, and fills the dark valley beyond with a light that is both gentle and awesome, then lifts, lifts, broadening and warming to diaphanous gold tinged with whites and vermillion. We become motionless. I want to thank Dad for not allowing me to miss this first light. He has closed his eyes as though to concentrate more fully on breathing in the splendour. And the sky blooms into a euphoria of frosted blues. The sun feels itself out into the earth.

The ascent of Becs de Bosson beckons, the last mountain of the three we are climbing this week. The six of us gather outside the hut's entrance, on the whitewashed veranda, and are silent. We know each other well, though we do not know the details of each other's lives. Rucksacks are hauled on, strapped around chests and waists. Ready.

I imagine Dad frantically rummaging for the blister plasters he has been mislaying every morning. When he emerges, we set off cheerfully. The sun, edging above the distant snowy mountains, wears a clarion shroud of phosphorescence for our final ascent.

Gornergrat Snow

Tomorrow we will meet the guide, the others in our group, at 7 a.m. beneath the clock tower. For now, Dad and I are content lazing through the adjustments in altitude and simply being together in a new place. I will always be his child and yet today we behave more like brothers, companions. Swifts bolt and glide down the main street, wheel up, quivering like flung ebony arrows, their fluttering style extravagant in comparison to the pared-down flight of two buzzards higher up above the town, sojourners of the sky. In threes and fours the swifts squeal, screech, and tumble headlong over the chapel, then burst away behind buildings, out of view, only the shrill calls still heard. We sip water from a stone fountain, and upon a mauve wall read a plaque dedicated to Edward Whymper, the sides of our interested faces almost touching. Dad's beard bristles lightly against my cheek.

Dad is intent on gaining a glimpse of the Matterhorn. I follow him along cobbled alleyways between preserved feed houses raised above ground on wooden plinths, and emerge at the village's edge. The top of the mountain is wrapped in scarves of unmoving cloud, its lower torso robust in its girth, and distant. In three days we will be sleeping upon its shoulder. It is Dad's favourite mountain.

I have never seen such a look in his eyes as when he beholds the Matterhorn.

Alpine choughs dive and rise in long lines above the Gornergrat glacier, their dark wings swishing through the cool air. From the south, mist is making its unstoppable way here, a lookout station of 3,027 metres, gliding and accumulating in mass, darkening from snow-white to dead-coral grey. Dad is busy inspecting alpine flowers as we amble over a broad ridge that takes us high above the glacier, towards the roof of the clouds. I have never before seen him so animated over flora and fauna. The rocks, too, their textures and burr, please him. He is gladdening company. A chill breeze starts to blow, snow-cold and laden with a weight of moisture, beading to our jackets, his beard and thick eyebrows.

We are the only ones sitting outside on a pale timber veranda at Gornergrat Restaurant. Snow begins to fall, and quickly thickens into a downpour of fat flakes that fall and twirl like petals of apple blossom or the moultings of snow geese. Halfway through our steaming tea, a waiter runs out and gives us each a navy blue blanket that we wrap around ourselves and drape down over our knees. The snow is heavy enough now to settle. I look across the table at Dad, who is smiling and laughing. Snow fills our tea glasses. Choughs as black as cinders, polished to a sheen, float noiselessly through the whiteout. It makes me happy to see Dad happy in the lily-white snow, the cascading white air. Our chests rise and fall beneath our blankets. The snow is as soft as edelweiss, his most cherished flower. I do not take refuge in myself as I have done in the past, only showing him the sides of myself he would expect to see. Snow sticks, melts into the weave of the coarse blankets. I urge myself to share in more of life with him, not to hold back, to really be a part of one another's blood. To be family not by mere name but by action and sense. The snow streams down, swinging to and fro. We are both open here.

Pfulroe, 3,300 metres

Wet fog prickles like sodden, hackled fur, and slides in great descending sheets heavily around us. At 3,000 metres the mist shifts, revealing a circle of blue sky through which the mountaintops poke. Up to our left beneath a dark cliff, chamois forage around the base of immaculate erratics. We watch the animals for a while, though they are far away. Their hooves clatter and tinkle through the scree.

Down to our right is an immense and austere glacial moraine, banked by long humps of grey stone, that runs from where the glacier ceases further up towards a close barrow of low cliffs above Zermatt. The moraine is haunted by the mood of powerful ice that has long since vacated. An enormous grave for a giant element. Sharp yelps of marmots, their abrupt shrieks bulleting through the air, off rocks, in a pinging series of alarming echoes, jolt us to attention. We cannot see them, but their bleats belt out.

Dad is breathless, as am I. At the snowline reflected sunlight is as bright as burning magnesium. The sky is a blue dome of newly engineered aluminium. Scrambling up through tilting boulder fields, we find the surfaces of the rock are too chill to hold for longer than is necessary to gain purchase, our hands uninvited to linger. I watch Dad's left hand grip nodules, spears, edges of slab, while his right arm is out like a wing for balance, and see the intricate flexing of tendons, the pipework of veins, the crimping of fingers that crinkle the whorls of his knuckles into patterns that resemble the rocks. Then the hand releases from a support to move forward to the next low shoulder of stone in front, shaping itself ready for the edge it will grab, crawling through the air. We move closely astride the boulders and scree at a pace that, set by the guide, is not too strenuous but is nonetheless demanding.

Spider threads are moored from one boulder to the other in glistening gossamer patterns that, reflecting the sunlight above and the snow beneath, seem unreal and evoke pauses of puzzlement in us all. Even the guide is stopped in his tracks by the delicate networks of spiderwebs, an acre of reticulated iridescence, sloping down over the boulders to the darker regions below the snowline. We stare. Dad is cautious not to break the webs but in doing so he jeopardises his balance, and slips. I do not want to break the silken craftwork either, but it is unavoidable. The threads tear across our shins as we regretfully mow through them.

Past the boulders, the snow is biscuit-brittle, a marble crust impressed into cracked slates by the chipping edges of our boots. We ascend, in plodding switchbacks, up the curved side of the col, hugged between the mountain and a shaft of black rock that juts out violently from the snow.

Catching Dad's eye as he trudges gleefully up towards the summit ratifies the sense of joy we are all stepping into. I am not alone in being drawn on into the mountain, an inhaling of elation that strengthens as the legs weaken. The steady rhythm of breathing falters, altitude nags us into disarray, but the mountain is an anchor.

Dad and I lunge up together onto the summit, and step down onto ice-stiffened snow. I have to close my eyes in the blinding radiance. For a moment, I turn dizzy with exasperation, then open my eyes in a state of disbelief at the awesomeness of the surrounding vista. My body is blown open beyond coherence. My breathing is out of step with my heartbeat. My eyes seem to wince before the vivid silence from which my ears cannot flee. I look away from the delighted expressions of the group towards my own point on the horizon: a lapis cliff hung with snow. In concert with Dad up here, all I can muster is an embrace with him, unable to find some other human technique that speaks of the deep rapport I feel for him. Between two small thumbs of scree, a pair of blue asters tremble. Dad and I sip water from our flasks, and eat chocolate.

The descent will jar our knees, shunt our toes into the curve of our boots, will be arduous. We will toil back through the broken filigree of spiderwebs, and shimmy down scree to the yipping of marmots, then stride out along the path towards the Matterhorn.

Hörnli Hut, 3,260 metres

The hemp-brown rope rail, scuffed and whiskered by the traffic of countless hands, yanks taut under the weight of our ascending group. A metre in front of me the nightclub bouncer from Leeds, brought here by a restless yearning to revel in wild travail, stomps with the gait of wired adolescence. The sides of his jacket brush against protruding swords of gneiss and ophiolite rock. His breathing, though, is measured. Four metres behind me, Dad is alternating between uneven strides to close the distance between us and an almost static walk. He is cursing. He yells that it helps to fire him up. He seems angry at the mountain, the Matterhorn.

Clag boils up from behind arêtes in strobing acts of terrific surprise, sails in over us like the ghosts of grey pack ice, and pursues itself in lattice-wending purls as reams of unfurling fog chase themselves with unnerving speed. The mountain seems to know we are here. I walk thoughtfully and quietly. We wear the clag like baggy chain mail that thrashes around us, bellows out, and subsides. Though our feet are shuffling, the bannister of rope slackening and tightening, our movement seems at odds with the stationary power of the rocks. I look back and Dad isn't moving at all. The mountain is slipping away beneath him like a sand dune surfaced in black volcanic sand. Too soon he is out of sight. The rope rail is tugging back tightly, creaking in his grip, before sagging as it is released to low U dips that make me worry that he's lost. Then the rope tightens. Relief. I wait for him now, with an alarming pinch of conscience. The others proceed up into swirling torrents of mist. Standing in the acute arm bend of the zigzagging trail, my back against slick sedimentary rock layered like shelves of axe heads, I cannot hear Dad and his cursing. The clag, restricting vision to no more than a metre, is claustrophobic and eerie. Though the map indicates that I am standing upon the shoulder of the Matterhorn, waiting for Dad, I could be anywhere, nowhere. All I can hear is my breathing and the beating of my heart. Such small cacophonies as these punctuate the yawning silence with islands of respite. Enclosed in a box of creeping fog and walled in by seeping black rock, the ground beneath us seems to lose its stability. Dad always said that the Matterhorn resembles a crooked wizard's hat, an image that is too fitting for this spell of misplaced levitation. Dad, as far as I know, might be somewhere else entirely, traipsing up the steps into the far corner of another earth.

Watching him emerge, finally, from the coiling rolls of fog, still cursing and panting, into this confined and massive space where I wait, is mysteriously poignant. His familiarity is settling. Here we find each other beyond the categories of father and son, at the juncture where two lives converge. Together we ascend the last cut-back of the trail, into snowfall, as dusk and mist and snow concoct to make a fluid darkness like that of the sea at night. A single lit window through the darkness makes us pause. The hut.

Bella Tola, 3,025 *metres*

Saffron-rose light at sunset fans out, ray by ray of deepening orange golds, through the horizon of distant peaks, and lingers at the stone walls of the cabin, at the two rocks upon which Dad and I sit, dazed by the rapid morning descent from the Hörnli Hut and our dash, by train, from Zermatt to St-Luc. My mind reels with all that I have seen. We sit here in rest, sharing a bar of milk chocolate, tired and content. Lichens, ruffled like edges of worn carpet, gently effervesce into molten greens. My fingers move over them as though they were the ancient Braille of the land. Dusk encourages us to go inside the cabin, for our evening meal, for bed. We fall asleep before we say goodnight.

The next day. Blood-pink stains of Saharan dust are speckled throughout patches of east-facing snow. An alpine lake glistens, awash with flies as weightless as castings of grass seed. Dad is chatting with the guide. There is a lightness to the mood of the group this morning that is a rebellion against the heavy darkness of yesterday. A sense of camaraderie, of companionship, has naturally developed over the week, without intrusions and the pressure to know the ins and outs of each other's personal lives. We know enough of each other to know we can share in the walk, to expect no offence, to be at ease with one another. A moving community founded on a pattern of respect for where we are. Our desires concur here. I succumb to a filial happiness that is as concrete as the rocks. Thirty metres of harsh ascent shy of the summit, we stop and glug water. It is hot. Dad and I remove extraneous layers, as do the others, the guide. The massif to the south is an altar, the sense of which has been earned. Life, here, the pinnacled beginning of it, has come full circle and brimmed. I am as close to Dad as I will ever be.

Becs de Bosson, 3,149 metres

Scree, like shattered slabs of honeycomb, crunches under my heel, rattles free, skitters down over the ledge of a precipitous ravine, the sounds of the shingle shower swallowed by the falls of silence. We are looping around stands of sedimentary rocks too brittle to gain confident purchase, our hands crimping hesitantly, heads ducking under arches, bodies squeezing sideways through clefts dark and cool. The mountain is an almost vertical maze with obstacles at every turn. The palms of my hands are dusted with the grain of the stone. The mountain is being entered into person by person, each member of the group exercised into it through a game of touch-and-go, hide-and-seek. It is like wandering through an elaborately structured home, drawn in further in search of the hearth, its centre, down corridors, through rooms and hallways designed to lose you in itself. The architecture of the mountain is deeply playful. I cannot get enough of it.

At the foot of a three-metre wall of bright schist, we hoist one another up by the rungs of foot and thigh onto the summit, which is too narrow to accommodate more than one person at a time. Dad goes first. His strong hands seek rock holds as I and another push him upwards from underneath his boots, our hands cradled around his soles. He kicks and scuffles up, and propels himself onto the summit. He steps out of sight, into the blue sky. I hope up there he takes all the time he really needs to let where he is and what he is sink into him and lift him out. Our waiting for his call to help him down is like the aftermath of a prayer.

Barrage de Moiry

On a fatigued high, the week's trek over, the group returned to their workaday lives, Dad and I stay on for one more day, to catch the bus from Grimentz to see the Barrage de Moiry: a sparkling blue reservoir, we are told by our hotel's receptionist.

Glacial blue water laps steep edges bordered by chest-high flowers that nod under the weight of bumblebees and butterflies. At the far end of the reservoir a gold-grey stream cuts down from luminous fields of snow. It is too cold even to touch. Deftly noticing that we are father and son, a lone woman with short dark hair and green eyes takes a photograph of us. We stand at the stream's edge. His left arm rests around my shoulders, and pulls me into him.

Upon a café terrace built into the top wall of the dam, we gaze out across the reservoir, towards the mountains. The day is turned to its highest intensity of colours. Crystalline blue and summer-grass green flowers, the bright white snow, the blue of the lake. Whilst drinking iced tea, Dad hands me a sprig of edelweiss, ivory-green coated with a diaphanous fur, which he nabbed from a flowerpot upon the café's exterior window sill. It is symbolic of so much I cannot fathom. A gift I marvel at. We break bread amidst bright flowers.

The day after tomorrow the demands of the daily nine-to-five will sap his energies, close him up. We will be pulled apart. If we are not careful, this week will dwindle into something inconsequential. We will flounder, prisoners of marginal existence, in scripted hours maintained by society's curriculum of profane toil. I imagine the land will be elsewhere, this week of mountains an impossibility.

Dad, let's not allow this walk to pale away into a mere holiday, an unreal foray. Let's not forget what holds us. I will put the sprig of edelweiss in a safe place.

The Beech Tree

One mile south from my home, in the New Forest National Park, stands a beech tree. *Fagus sylvatica*. To reach the tree I walk along a mud, sand, and white-flint track that takes me through ankle-high heather, past lone silver birches whose showers of leaves lightly clash in the wind, then into Studley Wood. Two moss and lichen-smothered timbers are poised either side of the path like remnants of a noble gateway. Beyond this, the path disappears beneath thickly overlain carpets of leaves and twigs. It is here that I remove my boots, tie them together by the laces, and drape them over my shoulders. As it is early September, with the sun entering through the wood in pulses and waves of mid-morning light, the ferns are head-high, and of a jade-green so bright as to be almost translucent.

Irrespective of the number of times I have walked barefoot into Studley Wood, almost every day through winter, spring, summer, and autumn, I always make my way to the beech tree. It comes into view like a home. When I first found it I was stunned not only by its elegant shape, the curving reaches of its branches, its leaves, but by its spaciousness. Not merely the space it took up within the wood, pushing the oaks and the ash away from its centre, but the space it gave beneath the nave of its branches, the column of its trunk twisting ever so slightly towards the sky, the profuse measure of its crown. Under its shelter, I experienced the same sensation of looking out to sea from a headland. Immensity. Room enough to feel the immensity of things. The openness of the universe. And the tree was my invitation to step into a space in which the divide between myself and the wood dissolved. Everything glimmered.

So it is that I return to the beech tree most days, not to try to relive that first experience but to allow the tree to become an essential part of my life, to steadily inform my habit of being, my *habitus*. Placing my boots to one side, I sit upon the ground and admire the tree, slowing my breathing to the pace of the wood, quietening myself, loosening my awareness, listening, vigilant. Somehow, through the beech tree's influence, I grow into another, fuller and more real mode of being. In that shift in consciousness, the tree seems to vivify into a presence, a living presence as commanding to my attention as a loved one. Not merely a tree with a name, only looked at as a picturesque scene or something of interest and potential use. I know now that the tree is sacred, not only through the intricacies of its biological functioning, the role it plays in the wood as provider of life to sky and soil, but also in its nameless being, the light it is unto itself. I address the tree in reverential silence, an attitude not put on consciously but elicited, naturally, from the tree itself, an attitude continuous with the exhalations of oxygen from its leaves, the rhythmic movement of water into its roots.

Each time I walk home I am changed, though I often cannot say how. For a while something essential is revived. The beech tree stands bright, breathing, and tall.

A Nocturnal Pact

Grass munched flecked with earwigs,
hoverflies that tremored amazed us more
than hawks tethered to god's sky hand of blue.

Brothers dream of being brothers again
where the paint-faded fence met the house
and in that corner, kneeling in dock leaves,

you stepped up onto my back hurling yourself over,
down into the neighbour's weird arena.
Strange and unforgiving you returned changed,

slinking away into obscurity with growing pains.
I hear your screaming coda
from where you must have vanished to:
further off than I could ever imagine.

I stand here where cobwebs shake
and ivy grips the vertical brick.

One Week in Arkansas

The Embrace

I waited for him at his home on a bright Friday beneath an October maple tree turning its roseate leaves in a silken wind. Jet-lagged, I dozed in a picnic chair facing the first morning warmth of the sun. Holding a mug of tea in my lap, I drifted in and out of sleep, to the tapping of the maple leaves above and the dancing of light upon the ground and on my eyes. Around noon a huge bird flew overhead, casting the shadow of its wings down through the maple tree, blending momentarily with the wing shapes of the leaves, crossing the sun, wheeling up higher and higher with ease. With my right hand shielding my eyes from the sun, I could begin to make out the bird's characteristics, the length and dark greys of its plumage, its particular gait in the air, and a thin line of glinting white-silver along its wing tips.

Before I went into the house to tidy up my room, the blast of an approaching truck horn shook me with complete surprise. It was my brother, home from a long haul to Colorado. He had been away for two weeks but I hadn't seen him in five years. Instead of rushing out to see him, I walked into the room to make the bed as though I was in denial that it was actually him. But when the horn, even louder, boomed so that the thin walls of his home trembled, I left the pillows and the sheets to make themselves, and paced outside. I didn't anticipate that I would be nervous seeing him again after all this time, but as he rolled the truck into the yard, brought the rumbling engine down to a purr, yanked the brakes on with a yelping screech, stepped down from the other side of the cabin, slammed the door, walked round the front of the truck, and saw me, I burst into tears. We held each other. He felt as strong as I remembered. Through the tears we let go, and he pointed up at the same bird I had watched earlier, now floating high above us in the blue sky, and told me it was a turkey vulture. And we watched it together, as it stayed above us for a few more moments, beat its broad wings, and then drifted over a pine wood towards the sun, diminishing to an incredible speck of life.

Coyote and Fire

As I gathered chopped wood from the barn for our evening fire, I thought back to when we were children making fires in the back garden, tearing branches off trees, conjuring clouds of smoke, warming stones to hold through the frosty nights or as long as we could before we grew tired and Mum or Dad called us back into the house for supper or bedtime. How many days and nights we spent being pioneers of our back garden I lost count, but they are written down in our history together, relived and renewed in those rare moments when, grown up, brothers give each other the time to feel, again, the kinship of childhood, the small adventures, the stories told as they are acted out. So I relished the fire on our first evening together, the gathering and assembling of the kindling under the stars that have seen out our lives with a lofty, tending patience, back from his porch, away from the maple tree, thousands of miles away from the garden where we spoke our first words, crawled, and learned to walk from the door to the apple tree, from the apple tree to the far hedgerow, from the hedgerow all the way back to Mum and Dad, candle flames flickering in their eyes, their hands gloved in care, their voices as wise as windows onto the wind.

The fire did most of the talking as we sat on sunken chairs an arm's length apart and quietly surveyed the fire, the sparks, and the stars. The shadow of the fire rode up the corner of the house and seemed to swing like a child from the eaves, doing pull-ups, swinging from side to side. Crickets crackled from inside the surrounding darkness, the areas where the fire could not reach to illuminate, and broke into a chorus at times, then faded away to leave a single cricket ratcheting a solo to the night, stranded beneath the stars with nothing but its anthem.

I cannot recall what subjects we broached except for my constant wonder at his new home, a wonder that shook with thrill when the sudden calling of coyotes froze the night tight and all was made to listen. In excitement I stood up as though beckoned to attention by the abrupt, raw, howling cackles of the coyotes in the near field. How far away were they, really? Could they see us, smell us, hear our fire? How far had they roamed to gather in that field of scrub, ponds, and tall grasses? Hearing an animal like that for the first time, a predator I had only read about and seen pictures of, jerked me out of what I thought were intensely embedded moments by the fire to an even more intense beckoning of life, to an immediate primal realm breaching the surface, raising its eye to mine. My brother remained seated, listening to the horde of wails, turning his beer bottle between his finger and thumb. I stayed on my feet and strayed towards the yard's edge, beyond the firelight into the night's quarters, and as I approached the boundary I heard what seemed like a thousand paws scampering over hard earth, thudding like hooves into further darkness. My heart drummed as though their paws pounded across it. If I had not strayed, and he had stayed where he was seated, they might have called all night.

Midnight came, my mind still fresh with the thrill of the coyotes, my nerve endings yanked open, and we grew tired towards the early hours. The warmth of the fire definitely reached him too for he had laid his hat, gloves, and jacket on the ground. Light from the fire gave his eyes strength enough to see the pine cladding of his home and the stars blinking along the spine of the roof, his cat's eyes amongst them perhaps, and to read the beer-bottle label as he picked and dog-eared its corner. Around 3 a.m. we retired to bed, thickly reeking of smoke. The next morning I wandered out barefoot through the vanishing, sunlit beads of dew, knelt and blew upon the still-warm mound of ashes. Ashes flew up, followed by trickles of smoke. Then, with an encouraging little triangle of dry sticks and more blowing, the fire revived, and regrew to a decent enough size for me to sit by and sip my coffee, thinking of the night before and of the days ahead, leaving my brother to rest.

The Truck

My brother had loads to haul. I was excited to be going with him. Three days out on the road, collections and drop-offs in Missouri and Kansas, then back into Arkansas. I washed out and refilled the water bottle, stuffed snacks into the deep side pockets of the doors, threw my bag on the bed at the rear of the cabin, and waited in the passenger seat for my brother, who was giving the outside of the truck a thorough inspection before we set out.

His cabin was small, hardly enough to accommodate us both. The duvet was crumpled in a pile and two pillows lay in an X in the far right-hand corner beneath a shelf overflowing with tinned foods, torches, cables, cards, photos, and other items. I imagined him lying there, alone in the night, halfway through a haul to Nebraska, pulled over on an anonymous dirt road linking up two towns 500 miles apart, and a strong winter wind blowing for ever and unimpeded across the prairies like waves, without a single obstacle rising and rolling across the Atlantic. Is he warm enough? What does he think of? Does he think of England, Mum, Dad, and me? Does he feel lonely? Questions, curiosities, worries reeled through my head as I nosed around the cabin, flicking through the oil-marked pages of his logbook, running my hand over the coarse interior of the grey vinyl sides, fumbling through brass tools that spilled out like treasure from the glovebox. After making his bed, swiping my right hand over the bedsheet to smooth out the creases and sweep off bits, tidying up as sensitively as I could without disrupting his organised chaos, I slumped back down in the high chair that elevated and depressed on squeaky springs and swung from side to side to afford me a view through the cinematic windscreen. Dusk moved in, bringing thick, opaque fog in its wake, and we set off in a thunderous lurch through the oncoming night. He looked back at the house in the rear-view mirror but it was gone inside a world of fog and evening darkness.

Hours passed in a steady motion as though the truck itself towed time. We talked a little, mainly about the places we passed through, what they looked like in broad daylight. Heading north to Missouri along a highway free of traffic,

I could make out the margins of huge lakes either side, reflecting a blurry medley of stars as we sped past. I imagined that they were as big as seas with their own weather and enough water to drown England. I spent time, too, watching my brother handle the forest of gearsticks that shook under the powering grind of the engine, and hold the globe-round wheel that spanned the width of his chest. His knuckles drained to white as his strong hands gripped the wheel at a turn, reminding me of his expertise with machines. Even as a child, he would busy himself under the flickering light bulb of the garage as Dad brought him some engine part to fix, feeling the pressures of an emergency like a surgeon.

We parked up for the night in the dock of a Flying V gas station, the engine left running to keep the heating on. The lot's floodlights made the sheen of the clean chrome of the hundreds of trucks a blinding glare, and I was glad when we finally drew the small curtains across the windows. We slept head to toe and, as he promised, the slumbering grumble of the engine soothed me to sleep. I awoke to him sleep-talking, and to the slamming of doors outside, deep resounding voices, the gearing up of engines as the trucks, in the early hours, crept forward from their resting places and slid, one after another, onto the highway, driven by bleary-eyed truckers roaring home or trundling further away. Where was my brother most at home?

The next morning, I watched the sun rise up through the skyline of Kansas City from the forecourt. The skyscrapers gleamed in the sun, and the dark blue of the predawn sky lightened to a silvery cyan flecked with striations of roughly hewn cloud. Kansas City diminished out of sight like the land of embarkation on an ocean voyage, and the horizon of infinite cotton fields beckoned.

The amount of space, the immense sky that dwarfed the largest span of land, was almost exasperating, too much to take in. Vast flat lands of identical fields were at odds with the small cabin that held us as we hurtled slowly south. There were no middle distances or features to negotiate between the extreme nearness of the shared space with my brother and the extreme far-off space outside. With the speed at which we moved, the fields turned into a level green sea, and I could do nothing else but glaze over and find rest in sleep's dark balm. How did my brother keep awake and maintain such feats of stamina in this rush of disorientation? I tried to stay awake with him as in a vigil, but an unbeatable sleep overcame me as I hunkered down in the cushioned chair, taking one last look at the road reeling into us and drifted off, my chin upon my chest, arms folded as though to hold myself together.

After three nights and two full days we arrived home an hour after dawn, when the morning mists brushed away from the hickory and the pines and dissolved imperceptibly into the cool air, leaving the light to caress away a weakly riveted frost. Trees dripped like a slow rain was falling, just a handful of drops. More leaves had fallen from the maple tree. A small blood-golden pile of them lay at the trunk, wet with deceasing frost. We collected our things from the cabin, the bed left unmade, the water bottle half empty and lolling on its side, and jumped down upon the sturdy ground that seemed to meet my feet with a clasp of welcome relief. Our doors swung shut in unison. My brother went into the house to shower, to wash his clothes, whilst I wandered around the yard, the sun upon my chest, hearing still the ringing rumble of the engine in my ears.

Creek and Mountain

The Ozark creek, sneaking down through narrow granite cliffs, was an icy turquoise and the sun, spliced by trees, irradiated the surface, the depths, and the pebble bed. We toed the water. It was burning cold.

My brother laid down on the stone bank, his legs outstretched, his arms out either side to prop himself up. Sunlight fell upon him, throwing his long shadow over the water and up the overhanging bluff above. Reflected bands of light shimmered up and down the rock on the far side. Despite the temperature, the water was irresistible so I stripped and waded out into the centre of the creek, away from my brother's shadow, into a pool of light that was warmer than I expected. Like a slow baptism, I lowered myself down inch by inch. The water flowed around me, splashed up against the clean grey cliff blemished here and there by splattered lichens, red, yellow, green, and black. I dunked down, breathless at the push of the water around my lungs, submerged my shoulders, then brought my head into the polar sapphire liquid, opening my eyes on the underwater world of silent golden light flickering upon the creek bed with its thousand bullion pebbles.

My brother had fallen asleep in spotlights of sun upon the shore. I looked at him for a while. In the afternoon, walking from the creek, my brother took me to the highest point near his home: Sugar Loaf Mountain. Its bulky, lopsided mass of sand-coloured outcrops poked out above the treeline, and over the creek. Through the thick forest of pine and hickory, we followed a path of soft soil and pine needles right up to the face of Sugar Loaf, which abruptly rose up and leaned over us at the height of 600 metres or so. Turkey vultures silently circled the summit clockwise. I followed my brother closely as he led me through narrow, ascending gullies of sediment up and around the mountain in spiralling zigzags. The grooves through which we scrambled were like deep, sliced scars in the body of the mountain, runnels of shadow, cool and secret. In the quiet of the gullies I could hear only my breathing and the scuffing, rapid footsteps of my brother. Clumps of brittle red sand fell away as I held on to them for grip, and rained down below, rasping into trees.

At a sudden turn of the cut path, with nothing but the endless blue sky behind, he stood holding out his hand, shaped to hold mine. He hauled me out onto the top, and I staggered upright. Then he began to run towards the edge of the mountain, at full speed, kicking up a low dust cloud behind him, and at the edge he leapt, falling away from sight, leaving a panic of silence stabbing through the air. I rushed over to the edge, thinking the worst, but there he stood, a metre or so down, the other side of the ravine. He was on his own summit, his arms pumped into a V of victory, crowned by turkey vultures weaving a halo of shadow around him. I didn't leap, but turned with him to face a vista of tree upon tree stretching to the horizon. I peered down the ravine he had leapt over, a dark chasm dropping 600 metres to the forest floor, and felt a breeze rise up from the darkness and pass between him and me as though the mountain itself were breathing. Turkey vultures rode in the whirring thermal it created. We stood gazing out into the distance, atop two summits belonging to the same mountain, separated from one another by a dark and deep fissure like two adjacent sections of human skull protecting the same mind. Below us the blue creek ran on into a wide river that washed away to a waterfall in the sky.

Last Night

On the final evening before my return home to England I ran south down the road to stretch out my body after three days of being cooped up in the truck with my brother, travelling from one delivery to the next across Kansas, Arkansas, and Missouri.

As I ran the road that reminded me of the English Hampshire lanes I was going home to – the lanes he hadn't seen in years – the sun's base curve touched the horizon, lowered, smouldered, flushed to the most fiery red I had ever seen, igniting the horizon into a long blade of magenta, then sank down in an easeful diminution of burning. Broad alfalfa fields, tall hedges of buckthorn, hawthorn, and cherry glowed in the sun's after-song of fading orange carmines and watery crimsons. The road darkened ahead, ditches turned into pits of shadow. The sky deepened to pitch-dark blue. First stars shimmered between the branches of a lone beech tree, clustering in its October foliage like rare golden fruits of the tree or the blinking eyes of nocturnal creatures.

I ran on into the darkening, hearing only my heavy footsteps slap and kick up from the loose tarmac. My breathing doubled as the road inclined to a fork diverging at a centre of tall grass and a dead hickory that resembled a splayed-out skeleton of shadow, its time-chewed branches pointing in all directions like a mangled compass. A few days before, my brother had taken me right, where the road narrowed to a rough track of tree roots and gravel that snaked around the back of the far fields, through an abandoned corn mill, across a parched creek, past a brown pond, and through a gap in the hedge of his yard. I now looked left and could see that the road led away further into the dark through an extended hollow of arching trees, beyond the fields and the last lights of houses, into the heart of elsewhere.

Creatures of the air and woods seemed to stir and draw near through the silence, a silence that had its own life, too, emerging from the finest to the most magnificent details. After another pause of listening and tightening my laces upon the footstool of a fallen branch, I turned and ran the straight line back to my brother's house, treading along the horizon of the road, turning the world beneath my heels. Stars swung behind me, hedges and trees and fields blurred by, and all stopped still at my sight of my brother's eyes as he stood waiting for me at the turn into his home.

Last Morning

We heard the geese but did not see them at dawn on the misty river. Only the sounds of them drifting towards us, downriver, the water rippling with their secrecy, filling the awning of silence under which we stood untying the cords of the trailer from the borrowed aluminium boat.

We pushed the boat out, and rowed towards the geese that flushed, in a cacophony of honking and wingbeats and splashing water. Under the bridge a fisherman cast his fly, whipping back the line and whipping it forward in a long, seething S with a continuity that was spellbinding. The small thin boat rocked as we shifted from right to left trying to get comfortable for our morning of fishing. We threaded the lines through the eyes, tied the hooks, fixed on the Powerbait, and cast our lines in concert. The reels whizzed then shuttered to a stop as the weight struck the bottom. Water beads garlanded the lines; each bleb held an individual hoard of light. The sun was warm upon our backs, the cool mists long gone, the trees were on fire with the artistry of autumn.

I was leaving to go home that afternoon but tried not to think about how long it would be before I would see him again.

Each thing, every quiver of the line, the water glugging against the boat, the stillness of a far-off heron that resembled a man, the dragging of the concrete anchor block along the riverbed, the slight touching of our warm backs, the odd word, the reeling in and recasting of the line, the fragments of bait dangling from the shining hooks, seemed to merge into a single motion.

Around noon we called it a day. The boat scraped up onto the bank and came to a halt. The paddles tumbled onto the deck floor. We threw the rods into the back of his car, and he drove me to Little Rock Airport. We talked about the week gone, the weeks ahead for each of us, the next visit home. We waved goodbye in October's last sun; the dream of its return already under way.

The Mute Swan

He was like the first paper aeroplane I made
then left out in the night: hefty with damp,
scrunched and chilled by strangling fists of dew,
rolling and slapping upon my heaven's beach

with every flow and undertow of morning tide.
Water burst out like kettle steam through a hole
in his chest as if from a stranded whale's
blowhole. Who could shoot a mute swan?

Was it some suspicious fisherman blaming
him for the year of no fish? Or did lightning
sear out the numinous flashing of his heart?
His time on earth was up, up, and down.

I dragged him by the turgid hose of his neck
through shells and sand. His wings, shrivelled
by salt, snapped back when I unfolded them
to the broad expanse they once were. Wind

rustled the once cashmere down of his feathers
now constricted by cuffs of crust. And the smell:
egret breath, faecal, sulphuric. Guava-like blood
dribbled from the winter-wheat grain of his bill.

The ingot seed and flare of his eyes were now
pinches of mustard white. It was a staggering
commotion when he laboured to fly in an attack
of every wingbeat. Turnstones, busy in the kelp

mats, scattered in alarms of ear-piercing bray.
Torso of a marshland angel, caved-in and stunned
by vice of wave and star, forgive me that all I
could do was bury you in what I know: root foyers

worming beneath a twisted oak. I firmly believe I
too will be bored through, hollowed out, hauled
into your nest of sky and twigs where you'll be clamouring
with the sun in your bill to put it where my heart is.

Impact

Once, in October, when I had stayed with you all weekend, I called your name, Mark, in the long dark burrow of the main barn. I moled my way closer for a glimpse of you or at least a reply to my call. The silence buried sounds in its depth. I listened deeper into the dark to find what the silence was hiding.

Outside, the autumn light waned in a slow swipe of dusk's cloak as it sank down and glided over the ground. I watched dusk shape the trees, and envelop the sky, soak across the courtyard past the barn door, priming the world for night's black coating.

I stood in the closed eye of the barn, and listened. The barn was darker than the darkness outside, and the silence within was deeper than the silence without. I shuffled blindly through the thick half-door. Its new bolts and hinges, though golden brass in the day, were pale pieces of darkness like bone in shadow. I called your name again. The silence grabbed the words and blanketed them. The silence hid you. The air was fragrant with old hay littered across the rough concrete floor, and in the corners there were fallen stacks of dry manure. A water bucket rolled away from me in an arc as I tripped into it. I abruptly put my hand out onto a low beam for support.

The barn was a ward of forgotten things, where the wastes of time wasted away in a time of their own. A rake, its clawed prongs snapped off, stood propped up against the wall. My fingertips moved in small waves over the coarse skin of a discarded saddle hung from the wall upon a long rusted nail. Another layer of silence added itself to the echoless depth and throughout, as I listened closely,

I heard a sweeping and swishing. My eyes have gradually adjusted to the dark. A bulb, wrapped in a spider's web, the spider dangling in the light, flickered from the pitched roof, shedding a wavering series of shadows down upon you and the horse you groom. *Impact* was that horse's name. The horse you loved so much the love felt like grief.

Chequered in sound and darkness, silence and light, you and the horse were very still except for your right arm, moving up and down, up and down, the curved side of the animal. She kicked her back left leg onto the ground, and jilted her head. She snorted, grunted, and backed away one step and you gently coaxed her forward towards you by the bit.

You passed me a brush in silence. We combed the animal together. Not a word was spoken. The animal breathed deeply and slowly. Her body was warm, and golden in its darkness. She was everything.

The Seal

One November, above Watergate Bay, the north Cornish sky was brain-grey and had the stare of an eye blinded by cataracts. Waves, caught between the incremental swell behind and the bucking roller in front, rose toppling to see the shore, the serpentine cliffs. Spray peeled free from the hunched backs of the waves, and hissed away towards the horizon, seeming to unburden the sea of an extraneous layer. The waves then towered to crests with torrential edges that steamed like dry ice, curled, and fell into their shadows, booming to the beach in thunderous flows. The power of the Atlantic was pumped into each wave, the gathering energy of it in the trough between them. And yet despite such brute force, the sky's blank agony, locked in a mute regard of its own colourlessness, was not relieved. The Atlantic was compensating for the dreamless impairment of the sky, hardly a sky at all; an overwhelming neutrality.

A pair of oystercatchers, huddled at the tideline, examined the sand. Their rowan-red bills, sticks of crimson crayon, were gorgeously apparent against the raucous greys and whites of the water. I was disappointed when they dashed into the air and skittered away to the east, leaching the last syringeful of the day's lifeblood in their bills. Flapping along the cliff edge, a crow tried to outdo a haranguing of gulls. A tired war of anaemic winged shadows took place on the cliff wall like a scene from a lethargic play, which gave more bite than the bodies themselves.

Sitting on a rock in a cave mouth, out of a limp easterly wind, it became more apparent that the day was chock-full of resistances that prevented me from breaking through into it. As a child I would often have nightmares like this.

The world would harden to brown iron and draw itself away from me, diminishing to an extremely distant star encrusted with an ashen hue, opening up an enormous gulf of flatness between myself and it over which I hung, briefly, then dropped. Wakened by my own screams, I would run across the hallway into my mum and dad's room that was made unfamiliar, the walls too high, the floor sunken, the light sickly. As Mum held me, my skin felt rock-hard, my mind jammed with expanding concrete, my gums ached. The world refused me. I shrank into myself as the world contracted away from me. It would take hours before the world softened again to accept me, to let me be included in my rest.

Quite close to where I sat, a dead and bloated Atlantic seal pup, mottled and ailing, floated upon a rock pool, covered with strips of glistening seaweed. On its back, with its flippers stuck straight up to the sky, it rocked slowly from side to side in the advancing undertow of the sea that had given up trying to revive it. I wanted to go over and inspect it but the tide was rising, and the pool brimmed and spilled through the rocks, submerging barnacles that blistered a chalk-white. The seal, eventually, was tugged out by the waves. I watched it buoy and bob out into the distance as I retreated from the tide towards the cliffs. I had never felt so far from things that day except in my recurring childhood dream.

On the tide-narrowed beach I was told by a listless dog walker that the day was going to brighten; the sun easing through like a painful realisation, a supine reprieve. I wanted to believe him. Indifference reigned.

Young Rain

A young rain has fallen.
With all the fragments that remain
what picture would you choose for me
to piece together?
I have a picture in mind.

Your factory gone to waste,
lovingly abandoned. Skips and cranes
on their sides. Ballast sacks empty
of all metal contents, wind-folded,
cast out of sight.
The car hill reduced to a wheel rolling
across the yard. Dust ghosts
swirling around the coffin baler. Sparrows
tumbling down from telegraph poles,
washing their backs in pothole pools.
The steel armoured gates shut on lorries,
voices your father introduced to you
finally interrupted.
A silence restored like no other.

And you are there, Dad, an old man,
bending down to the boot-riven ground,
where brass and oil would've smeared the tarmac,
holding up a single growing grass blade,
tilting it towards the sun.
This could be a sign of peace with the earth.
A young rain has fallen.

Collections

I waited for Dad on the roadside, holding two takeaway coffees, below the neon white and green column of a BP garage sign. This was our pickup point, every Saturday throughout the year at 6 a.m. I was in the first year of university at Royal Holloway, bewildered and homesick. Rather than working behind the student bar or waiting tables in a quarter-full café in Egham or Staines, I was relieved to be helping Dad collect and sell on metal from a Heathrow demolition site, what would later become Terminal 5. The scrapyards had become too much to manage; the late hours, the unfair pressure of maintaining an increasing family business required too much from Mum and Dad's relationship. The physical strain had taken its toll on Dad's health. They decided to downsize. No staff, no premises. Only Dad and Mum deciding their own worthwhile contracts. Ships and factories.

Like a truant, I loved dipping out of student halls at 5.30 a.m., escaping the rigmarole confinement, wearing a familiar set of work clothes that made me feel grounded and found, passing bickering and drunk late-nighters loitering at the closed doors of the bar, the claustrophobia of the ordered library, the weight of it all, to meet Dad, stepping into freedom. On those walks to meet him, when Venus sparkled like a lantern of aspiration above the lid of suburbia, I could breathe again. If I was early or Dad was late I would peruse the headlines of newspapers displayed in their open caskets along the front of the garage, or perfunctorily flick through the pages of a textbook, showing willing to myself. Rush hour began hours earlier than it used to. I wondered if people ever went home.

My spirits lifted when I spotted his flatbed truck emerge at the top of the hill beneath the iron-wrought bridge, seeming to pause on the mellow brow as though Dad faintly applied the brakes in order to see me there, in the near distance, in a framed moment of stillness. His son. The truck careered down the hill, the bundle of ratchet straps and heavy-duty tarpaulins crashing around loosely in the back, screeching to an exaggerated and bumpy halt on the kerb as though we were taking part in a heist. He raised his thumb to me through the window in a gesture that said, *You made it, you're home.*

To get here for 6 a.m. he'd leave home at four thirty, putting on his work clothes in the lamp glare of the hallway outside the bedroom so as not to wake Mum, seating himself on the outskirts of the round pine table in the kitchen alcove, the arena of countless family meals. He'd then collect his bag from the coolness of the utility room, grab his bundles of keys from the white window sill beside the front door. The truck purred and rumbled as though discordantly participating in the first waves of the local dawn chorus. Before driving north up the chestnut- and beech-lined avenue, he'd swing round to the clifftop, and gaze out between mirror checks and gear shifts to the horizon of sea cupped between the chalk edges of the Isle of Wight Needles and the Old Harry Rocks of Dorset; a view that was as much a part of me as the house. When I clambered up into the truck, setting the coffees into their holds in the dashboard, I was home; he brought it with him in abundance. Dad, a harbinger of return, briefly held my shoulder before turning off the kerb, jarring the suspension, joining the commuters.

At the demolition site, the sun rose through acres upon acres of piled rubble, illuminating the separated stacks of copper and lead with the glow and glint of treasure. The sight of planes, docked in their hangars for repairs, waiting on the runway, casually hauling themselves into the sky with turbulent laughter, others passing, dropping, gliding to earth with mesmerising skill and smoothness, the people ferried away and ferried home, lent a definite thrill of adventure to the morning's work. We must have seemed so small to the passengers as they turned their heads to the side and looked down, the ground we were on launching up through their bodies, the sky accepting them into the arrow of flight.

The reassurance from knowing that I'd be here again with Dad, watching the sun rise, the colours change, dragging bundles of cable-tied copper piping onto the truck, kneeling to take up one last plate of lead with Dad assisting, wincing as nearby planes blasted into life, ensured that I could take the week in my stride, that I had plenty to look forward to.

Watching from the roadside around noon, the sight of Dad's truck leaving over the hill was the beginning of his return to me. A week's journey, passing through home on the way, weaving an indispensable pattern like that of blood moving to and from the heart.

A Figure in the Doorway

I see my mother standing at the back door
in her long lavender gown.

She wonders what's become of this house,
seeing no clearer as long as she looks
through a few straggling hairs
that beat about her eyes.

The lawn has grown two or three inches
since the last gasp of rain.

The clematis and rose in the trellis
have petals to shed,
to be raked away as autumn leaves
and burned when he gets home.

Every day the same crow comes to pick and jab
his way amongst last night's
half-finished dinner for a family of four.

A cobweb glistens almost between table and chair
where we used to squeeze through
and run round to the door
that we opened because you shut it.

Now locked away in some warp of living things
that no memory can tally with,
you seem to fear the silence of what must become:

the hallway wilting into emptiness,
bumps rising like injuries in the carpet
because of a floorboard no foot
will step down flat.

You hang on watching a wind get snagged in the apple tree
like once when I saw from our speeding car
a white fawn tangled in a bundle of barbed wire.

Winter

The Tree

The tree and I meet by accident in sleep.
The dream begins when I am lifted
into its winter branches.
Still remaining upon the ground,
amongst beetles and leaves,
the tree hands me back to myself
along with something indescribably more.
Moss and light blossom in my hands.

Gifts

When I was too young to visit the scrapyard, Dad brought home ornaments for my brother and me. At some point, however, Mum put a stop to Dad bringing back salvaged gifts for her. Over time, the thoughtful knick-knacks deteriorated into unwanted tat. The fireplace and brick surround could no longer accommodate yet *another* antique gas lamp limbed with decorative butterfly keys or *another* pump-action blowtorch with nozzles like the barrels of a sawn-off shotgun. The kitchen window sills – heaped with gleaming copper kettles, pans with double-sided handles of rivet-fastened brass, grey ceramic jars decorated with wavy brown stripes brimming with arrays of old, dull coins ranging from shillings, farthings, mites, to coins of exotic origin – resembled overpacked shelving in a bric-a-brac shop. My brother and I would sneakily slip foreign coins into Mum's purse, removing the pounds and pennies, so that she ran into embarrassing difficulties at the local shop. She had to police the hoarding, keeping to a minimum our time spent with Brasso in one hand and a scruffy ball of wire wool in the other; a chore Dad never failed to dish out at weekends. My brother and I relished, however, all the oddities that Dad would bring home like artefacts from some distant land, pulling them from his bag like a magician.

One night, a week before Christmas, Dad arrived home with two ornaments that were particularly striking. After a long day of ice and iron, the headlights of his red Toyota pickup flooded the driveway through sheets of sleet, riding up the hedgerow, then extending as one long beam into the curtains of the living room slightly parted by our Border terrier, Ollie, as he yapped on hind legs in excitement at his master's return. Before Dad had even set down his bag upon the front step to remove his steel-toecapped boots, oily jeans, and thick black socks, he presented me with a shining tin model of a snake the size of a juvenile adder. He gave my brother a box of polished bullets and a clean gun shell that was longer than his own forearm. Gloating enthusiastically, my brother rattled the box too close to my ear.

We were in our pyjamas and felt the outside cold immediately. Mum, allowing us to stay up past our bedtime to greet Dad, rushed out from the kitchen, a blue and white checked tea towel slung over her right shoulder, and carried Dad's work clothes back through the kitchen into the utility room, handling them with urgent care as though they were precious robes. The powerful tang of Dad's oil-ridden clothes was as familiar to me, and as comforting, as Mum's perfume.

That night, I set the snake down upon my pine bedside table, surrounding him with a circle of little pebbles I stole from a jar of stones Dad had collected on our holidays. From tail to head, moulded into a rising coil like a spring trapped in the tension between unleashing and crouching, the snake glistened sunlit chrome in the lamplight. It glowed with an inner light. If I looked at the snake long enough, lying on my side, I would begin to doze as though hypnotised by the indent of its eye, and as I began to fall away into sleep, I sensed the snake coming to life, shifting from its metal form into a real animal. I would then, after this sense gained enough strength, open my eyes quickly to see if the snake was real, to see if it had slithered away or uncoiled itself into a taut, predatory line. But no matter how many times I tried this, the snake defeated me. The sense of its animation never faded, but catching it was like trying to see the back of my head without mirrors. The uncertainty of whether or not the animal would come to life when I finally went to sleep lingered in the air like an unfinished dream. I stayed up for some time, caught in this strategic game of hide-and-seek, and only really began to give in to sleep when the television went silent beneath my room and I heard Dad carefully stomp up the fourteen-step staircase, pausing on the landing for a brief moment before stepping up once more into his bedroom. I listened to the broken and muffled conversation between Mum and Dad as they talked with mouthfuls of brush and toothpaste, putting me at ease in the dark. Then their conversation flowed freely after the intense duet of baritone and alto gargling, and faded out as their bedroom door softly closed.

The next morning I woke early enough to watch, from the empty side of his bed, Dad leave for work. His pillow was still warm. The red tail lights of the Toyota were reeled into the dark by the pull of the dawning day. Sleet had turned to snow on the lawn.

Fort Fareham

Dad burst into the office like a hooligan, exclaiming that he'd not only seen a ghost but had also walked through it, and that the air had suddenly turned unbearably chill where the ghost had lingered. Having spent the morning cropping cable and working the baler, I was now with Mum in the brick and tin-roofed office, resting.

The office walls, painted slapdash in clotted-cream yellow, were smirched with cocoa-like stains of invading fumes and dust. Teardrops and long globules of paint between the brickwork made the walls look as if they were melting. Dad stood alarmingly in the doorway, the view of the yard stretching away behind him through a cloudy pane of fire glass. Forklifts were humming back and forth, weaving between workers who lugged tin-can bales and copper piping on their shoulders or rolled ten-gallon drums full of brass and bronze swarf, preparing, it seemed, for battle, swiftly moving ammunition and defences into place. Mum, used to Dad's frenetic outbursts about paranormal sightings, carefully slid a strand of her auburn-blonde hair away from her eyes and back over her head, and resumed tapping the calculator in the staccato rhythm of Morse code, logging numbers into books, their spines creaking as they were stretched apart. I stopped flicking through the year's calendar of 'Bikes and Ladies', pinned to the wall by one of the workers (much to Mum's disgust), and followed Dad outside, towards the location of the ghost, towards the miles of Second World War tunnels that ran beneath the yard in vast networks of haunting abandonment. His grey fleece hat sat slightly askew atop his head, one of its ear flaps lodged in the hat itself, exposing an ear to the February cold. His scuffed black boots kicked up from the potholed asphalt, large-looped laces flaying around his ankles. His arms swung back and forth with militant determination. Now and again he bellowed orders to his workmen or exchanged a variety of hand gestures that took on the complexity of sign language; a necessary means of communication when, in the main vicinity of the machines, every human voice was cancelled out by the roaring drone.

Operations, conducted through this signalling, seemed covert, full of conspiracy and espionage. The factory elicited its own language and dialect, expressed with quirky aplomb by the band of men who knew the terrain of the factory well, through every season of weather and trade, every slight shift in the stockpiles of wire and iron, and who met every change with trained efficiency.

We set off for the tunnels like a secret service, threading our way like shadows towards the growing darkness of the oval entrance. My brother was already inside, coming at us from the darkness, wielding a flashlight in his hand, breathing heavily, a hem of cobweb caught in his brown hair. So much braver than I, he thought nothing of jaunting off into the low concrete tunnels, following their passages that forked again and again, splitting into darker and darker corridors of oxygen-depleting silence, leading him further away from the yard towards what was, he imagined, the most top-secret place on earth, a government hideout or stairway into the fires and brimstone of an underworld. I did worry for his safety, though, as I lingered at the tunnel's entrance, calling his name to see if he was OK, putting my ear up to the echoless gloom, my feet inching their way over the border between light and dark. Even though he had mapped most of the tunnels in the surrounding area, he never actually found anything, except rats. One tunnel led up, he said, to a bunker that sat in the woods overlooking the yard from a cliff ledge. But he stopped going that way once he came across a homeless man lying face down on a ripped mattress, comatose and soaked in vodka.

'It was here,' Dad said, 'right here, that I saw him,' pointing with both hands in the way you might present an open book. 'He looked at me too. He was wearing khaki uniform, and wore thick-rimmed glasses. Come to think of it, he sort of looked like my dad. He was holding a clipboard out in front of him, checking off some kind of list with a pencil. He was so pale.'

'You saw a ghost, Dad?' my brother keenly interrupted, waving the flashlight on our faces. 'Wow! Maybe I should go back into the tunnel to look for him...?' My brother shimmied back into the darkness like a nocturnal creature, at home in the dank, retreating until his torchlight and footsteps were gone.

Dad was staring intensely into the space where the ghost had stood, reaching out and touching the air, feeling its absence, fumbling for a trace. He looked vulnerable, lost. It started to rain, the first drops tentatively pelting ten-gallon drums, a reconnoitre for the remaining troops of rain that arrived in incremental pulses before coalescing into a hammering downpour. Rather than make our way back to the main warehouse, Dad and I stood under the shelter of the tunnel, my head to his shoulder, our backs to the dark, looking out across the yard. Somewhere, my brother roved. Our breath plumed out from under the tunnel, rising, mingling, and disappearing into the rain.

Eryri

These mountains are my towering parents.
Y Garn, Glyder Fawr, Moel Siabod.
Their names go on and on
rolling like sweet snow upon my tongue
as my feet find footing in falling scree.

I hold the stones for a while at sunrise,
inhale the fragrance of Afon Glaslyn,
listen in on the erratic inner chamber of silence,

hearing deep and cloudy groans.
The space above the summits
shakes the heart like wind through winter rush grass,
the eyes are fraught bleary.

Ravens,
like children devoted to their parents,
carry conversations
back and forth between the mountains.

I doze in rain through many ages
below the ravens' continuous ferrying.

The heathers of Llethr Gwyn,
the lichens of Yr Aran.

The Ravens of Clogwyn Mawr

Gusts, racketing from the south, lash down the clag-shrouded flanks of Moel Siabod, pick up speed and uproar, then explode across the summit of Clogwyn Mawr. I am knocked down. A fifteen-stone man knocked down by a force he cannot see, but can hear in the wrestling heather. Pushed to crawl, I tuck myself away behind a fist-thick block of granite that's blotched with confusions of cabbage-white lichens. A familiar and much-used refuge during this tough vigil for the winter ravens. I am determined to see how they fare. The exertion is neither toil nor play, but is both of these plus something else entirely, something that I am hard pressed to explain, pummelled and whisked from the crucible of Eryri.

Facing north, I look out over the higher mountains of the western Carneddau range and say each of their names – Pen yr Ole Wen, Carnedd Dafydd, Carnedd Llewelyn – as my eyes scrupulously move over the plateau skyline, slope down into the lower range that is home to the austere waters of Llyn Cowlyd, then right up to this mountain upon which I wait, upon which my cold hands press. Clogwyn Mawr. The number of times I have performed this exact ritual has reached a tally in which the number is no longer relevant. Counting ceases when the mountains take over.

A hush bursts through as elemental as the wind itself, the held breath of the mountain. It is into this space that I expect the ravens – perhaps a singleton, perhaps a pair – to swing. But not so. The big hush is batted out as the gust blasts through. Directly overhead, a dragging board of grey-black cloud arduously slides north. Rain, enormous bows of rain, columns curling as they run, scraping ground and sky with their furthest tips, sweep through the cols and dissipate over the lowlands that are flooded by the bank-breached Afon Llugwy. Distant waterfalls look like avalanches, churning with horrific muscularity. In the corners of my eyes, now and again, I see dark specks appear and vanish. Hallucinations. A hail of wishes. A lie of ravens.

One hour passes. No ravens. The squall does not relent. I am soaked through. My hands are chapped from years of deliberate exposure. But I am settled. Over time I believe I have become increasingly joined to this land. It was not my conscious intention. Some places get into you, and that's that. You have to let them in, hand yourself over to the core. Every weather, season, nuance of scent, sight, taste, and texture are necessary expressions of the mountain and entrances into it. It all matters. I must step into it right. Giving in, folding, to this place is the appropriate etiquette, and I can have it no other way.

Every detail must be painstakingly noticed for my inclusion in the land. My vigil bolsters receptiveness, and the space into which the ravens may emerge trembles with alert expectation. I am wired into it, blood and brain, taut and ready like a coiled spring. Whilst the ravens are busy elsewhere, a rich meanwhile presents itself. Myself, the place, the bird that I am seeking are a non-linear, dynamic reticulation, budding with rhythms that are as slow as the lichen and as rapid as the wind. I immerse myself in that trinity and the connecting threads may – if I wait long enough – show a side of themselves I could never have guessed. So it is that I wait.

Down from Clogwyn Mawr, leaving behind the housing of granite, I tread – bent at the knees, my centre of gravity hooked down by the heather – to the edge of the mountain. If I stand too long I will be knocked over again, so I kneel and look out west to my destination: Clogwyn Cigfran. Crag of the Raven. The face of the crag bulges out past the surrounding cliff as though, in time, it may form the head shape of a corvid. An unfinished work of colossal masonry. Under the overhanging bulge are three gaunt trees: two rowans and one silver birch, gnarled, scabbed, and old. I have seen a raven fly out from those trees before but I have never found a nest in the branches or in the dark recess beneath the overhang. Once, in summer, the pale red light of the rising sun set the silver birch on fire with a flame that was crimson and silver, and caused the rowans to sink back into shadow away from their brandishing neighbour. Then, as the sun rose, and the cloud of pale red light became a flooding of pearly orange-gold spreading up over the unborn head of Clogwyn Cigfran, a single raven flew out from the crag itself as though unlocked from the rock by the key of the sun, and dived down towards the clear stream of Nant y Geuallt. Through my binoculars, I watched her bathe and preen. Her black feathers glistened in the shining cloak of water.

Again, I make my way over to Clogwyn Cigfran, scampering down the shallow cliff, following the line of the tumbledown stone wall to the three winter trees sleeping in a quiet agony beneath the roof of the raven cliff. Repeating and repeating my journeys, digging myself down into this land, grinding myself away on the edges of storm and stone to a fine point of self-effacement, honing myself to become ever more receptive to the faintest stirring in the air, is a necessary response to the beckoning of the raven.

I weave in and out of the three dripping trees, the thin rowans and the strong wisps of birch branches budding with raindrops that clip themselves free. Small pools of rainwater have collected in the rocks beneath. I look into them, hoping to spot some creature I have never seen. Rounding my way up the grassy bank that hugs the side of the crag, I am deep in the wind and the rain. Higher up, on the flat top of the crag itself, my back against a familiar lone erratic, kneeling, most of the high peaks of northern Eryri are visible through the squall, dark and punished by the weather, crusted with ice and snow.

The first peak I see is Moel Siabod and its rocky spine petering out to a boulder-strewn crown. Last summer I was at ease on that warm summit, watching a pair of ravens revolve like dark planets, the mountain the centre of a system in which every lichen, grass, and animal took part in an order of wild magnetism. I was lifted up amongst, them. The ravens alighted upon adjacent protrusions of granite that reached out towards the east, bearing their lichens and glacial scarrings like gifts. The ravens hopped from rock to rock, inspecting each deep gap, standing still, one behind the other and slightly to the left, closing and opening their eyes more and more slowly until I thought they had fallen asleep in the warmth. They sprang up, beat their wings, and continued wheeling around the summit in wide circles. The creaking whoosh of their wings through the air sounded like the repeated *whumphs* of a stove being lit and relit in a succession of tender ignitions. I then drifted into sleep, tucked between walls of rock on warm green grass, slipping into the mountains, into the silence of the ancient stone. When I awoke, the ravens were gone. They had the whole of Eryri in which to be abroad.

Further around to the south, the second peak I see is Snowdon, covered in dark cloud. This winter, up below the face of Clogwyn y Garnedd, I watched a single raven – extremely dark against the extreme whites of the wind-blown snow – take measure of its surroundings. I climbed up above the Pyg Track, out of sight and earshot of the trickle of crampon-laden walkers crunching and squeezing ice underfoot, and sat in a hollow of snow I dug out with my ice axe. I put off my desire to reach the summit, and made a cold afternoon of watching that single raven hang above the void that's cupped between joined mountains, each summit a knuckle of the mountain's shared hand. Ice fell from the ridge of Crib Goch that loomed above and behind me, clattering like broken porcelain shaken vigorously in steel pans, echoes fading as they rippled across the magnificent container of winter air. The wind cut down from the steep and pristine face of Yr Wyddfa – Snowdon – and whipped up disbanding globes of snow that blew over the raven as she sailed through the thickening whiteout. As the fog lowered, reducing visibility to no more than a metre, I could hear but not see her. A silence that is the silence of mountains, the winter silence that is Snowdonia's own, consumed the tinkling noise of the walkers and climbers below, consumed the features of the mountain, consumed my own eyes. In that cold blindness, the song of the raven's movements, the chiming whisper of her feathers somewhere in the white-iron fog, became larger than the land. The silence made her everything. And then, she called. A call like the clonking of mute bells struck with a spar of ice. She made that call again. And then she called out a note like the wobbling and buried twang of a slack guitar string plucked underwater.

The fog lifted slowly like a lid. I could see again the mountains and the snow, the dark rocks, the rigid waters of Llyn Glaslyn. And farther up, directly above me, I could see the raven as she flew effortlessly in the wind over the serrated edge of Crib Goch, and out of sight. I then made my way down the mountain, postponing summit glory for another day, casting an eye back now and again to spot, perhaps, the raven.

The third peak I see is the long and humpbacked mass of Pen yr Helgi Du. Last autumn, I was afforded ample time to study the profile of a raven as it accompanied me across the precipitous saddle of Bwlch Eryl Farchog. She darted out from a steep slope of heather and scree, and turned a sharp arc back around towards me as I was scrambling up the crest of Pen yr Helgi Du, trying to gain a whole view of her. Cloud shadows swept over the mountains. A soft golden light seemed to glow from within the rocks as the shadows passed. The wind was constant, coming in west from the Irish Sea. Resting halfway up the crest, I turned to find that raven hovering to and fro no more than two metres above me, framed against the moving canvas of cumulus clouds. No wingbeats, only acute tiltings of her wings and her body from left and right to realign her balance. She was more hawk-like than corvid, chiselled smooth to an angular and predatory shape. She rose methodically and with intention, following the curve of the rocky crest as I too made my way carefully upward. As I walked out onto the summit, another raven arrived from the far side of the mountain, hoving into view with an equal determination. They almost brushed wings as they flew past, croaking, then wheeled back around in mirror movements. They darkened and lightened in the alternating rags of sun and shadow. The raven that accompanied me rose high above the new arrival, then tumbled down and across in a rolling, random free fall. The second raven watched on, and rose up to follow the careless skydive until the first flashed out its wings and flew strongly to the ground, calling out in a tone of gruff announcement. The second, still remaining above, cork-screwed horizontally across the sky in a rapid acrobatic display of half-turns and dramatic wing dips. The first hopped up, seeming to get caught in the wake of the other's flight, hauled along with it, beak to tail. They both seemed young and full of life, making a riot of song, rimed with wizened grace, tilting this way and that, one in front, then the other. They knew one another, surely.

It is dusk at Clogwyn Cigfran and the ravens have not come. I make my way back to Clogwyn Mawr, to where this vigil began. It is foolish to think such time is wasted waiting for that bird. The raven's absence today is as compelling as its presence, in another form. As I pick out my route through stone and heather, dusk is made darker by the rain. I stop below Clogwyn Mawr, and wait at the fence line beside the ladder stile for one last time. Though the raven does not appear, I picture her there, garlanded in evening, beaded with rain, drifting west. Her call notes are the granite's song. And her silence is the dormancy of the forces that created this place through twisting aeons of ice and fire. She is the dark door opening and closing with every wingbeat through which I intimate that everything around me – the rain, the rocks, the evening sky – is held in place.

My imagined picture of the raven in the evening sky is washed away by the rain. My vigil is over. I climb the ladder stile, and traipse home.

A Cold Move

Chopping Logs

I became a neighbour to that father and son, my house sharing in the shadow of Raven Mountain, moving from a place where rainy days were rare and the norm was an evergreen wood below blue skies.

The house had been unoccupied for months. On the day I moved in, cautiously driving up the track banked steeply on either side with bracken, streams, and rocks, I saw the father again hunkered over an axe in the winter rain, chopping logs piled around him against the backdrop of the mountain. Though he nodded, he did not seem to recognise me as I passed him towards the gate of my new home.

The cut of the axe through lopped wood and my opening of the gate bolt occurred at the same time. Ricochet. I stepped through to my new home beneath giant clouds and with icy raindrops bursting open on the back of my neck. I looked out through the window at Raven Mountain, and followed the curve of its shoulder to where it met the eaves of the grey house that shimmered behind curtains of rain in its own dim globe of a world.

I watched the father wriggle the axe free with one hand from the support log. Rain dripped down his jacket in long threads. Hauling the axe head high, there was a pause in which the heather, grass, rain, rock, and sky rushed in to impart their power, then the axe swung down, slicing through the heart of the oak. He bent down and pushed aside the cut log with the back of his hand as though brushing away crumbs. He yelled out to the house, and his son, wheelbarrow in hand, ran over, the barrow collecting rainwater, the wheel jumping over stones. The boy started to load up the logs one by one whilst his father worked the axe like the hand of a clock striking at each hour, as though trying to cut into a deeper layer of time than the numbered days. The son was quick in his loading of the logs, but the father, in his anger, made him fumble. He hated the logs lying idly around. The son couldn't keep up and tripped on the asphalt, bashing his head to the ground, tipping the wheelbarrow onto its side, the logs spilling into puddles. He lay there in the rain, crying. Blood dripped from his forehead, down over his face. His top lip was split at the centre. The father shrugged his broad shoulders, either not caring or loosening his muscles before the next swing.

The Rabbit

I awoke to thunder rattling the yawning sky. The morning was dark. Hail clattered against the windows like thrown clout nails. No lightning, only thunder, deep and inmost to the sky, quaking like shook earth.

Between the splits of thunder there was the smaller, human rumble of the father yelling at his son, whose school uniform was splattered with blood. An exploded rabbit lay in pieces beside a double-barrelled shotgun. The dogs were yammering on their chains, which struck the tin roofs of their huts as they jumped and barked, jumped and barked. The father picked up the gun mid-barrel, grabbed the scruff of the son's collar, and dragged him through the hail into the house. The door slammed like a muffled gunshot. The son re-emerged wearing a clean white shirt, and ran down the asphalt drive to the lane beside the dark river, his slack bag swinging across his lower back.

A crow drifted down from the one tree in their fold; a threadbare pine shred by years of wind and rain to a drab skeleton of anaemic russets. The bird hopped forward, each step an eager inching, tilting its head from side to side to let its eyes see the bowels of the rabbit. Before its first peck the sudden rumbling of the rickety red Land Rover startled it away and it flapped back into the pine, cawing a scrawny peal. Red diesel filled the air. The father unhitched the tailgate, unclipped the dogs and whistled them into the back where they stood, panting. The Land Rover squeaked and trundled down to the lower fields where black sheep huddled together away from the swelling river, bunched up against the wall in a shivering clump of dark wool.

I went out and scooped up bits of the rabbit into a bag and walked towards Raven Mountain. The hail ceased. The wind was light but numbingly cold, the sky grey and hard like a sheet of iron. Sticking to the trodden line that hugged cliffs to the right, I reached the summit without resting. I tipped the rabbit out onto a snow-coated rock slab, backed away onto a lower shelf and waited behind the stone wall. Soon, two ravens swung into view and drifted above the kill. Their black coats shone out from the snowy rocks and the pale sky. One lowered, but then lifted again to be close to the other. They seemed unsure of the cache, sizing it up, taking stock. After drifting in and out for a while, their wings swishing in the breeze, they hovered down to the kill, and ate.

Deep in the valley the river fields had flooded from endless rain. The black sheep had been led by the dogs into a safer field. The father stood at the field's edge holding on to his crook, whistling and calling the dogs back into the Land Rover. He slammed the field gate into its latch, and drove home, turning slowly up the drive, then stopping at the barn and sitting there for a while, still and silent. The pine crow flew over to the roof gable, the branch perch unbending as though relieved of a burdening pain.

The Chase

Under a blue winter sky he talked about the state of his asphalt drive. Raven Mountain was in a bloom of snow. Pointing at bare sections of his yard, he spat as he talked about the price differences between asphalt, gravel, and tarmac. His voice resounded, a lode of anger beaded through the brunt of each word. The dogs, behind us, whined. The chains softly crashed against the walls of their tin huts as they trod from side to side through their own faeces, their tails and tongues wagging. Over the field from the base of the mountain the son came running, leaping over the barbed-wire fence that sagged between the fence posts. A feral dog had chased him, baring its teeth, in the woods on the lower slopes. The father drove his quad bike to the woods with his shotgun rested lengthways across his lap. Minutes later, the son, still panicked, stood beside me as we both looked out towards the woods in silence. An echoing blast cracked the tense moments into splinters. The father had shot the dog.

That was nothing, he told us when he got back. The son's eyes were fixed on the lower river, not on his father, who was bragging about drowning unwanted sheepdogs in chain-wrapped hessian sacks in the river, or shooting them without a second thought. The son retreated into the house as I said my goodbyes for that day. Far off from the weak blue sky, cloud-banked thunder was a distant rumble, as though the mountains were feeling out for themselves into the distance, lifting the horizons above their heads, dashing them to the ground.

I found the dog the day after, swollen and wan, a cavity through his skull, sunken in the river's side and pummelled by a small but a powerful waterfall that parted his cream back fur.

The View

The rain ceased, blew itself out. The air lightened, a high breeze touched by distant plateau snows rode up our backs, riffled through our hair and waved onwards, brushing the margins of broken bracken that danced like puppets searching for their strings. During the climb, we took rest at random intervals. The father was watching us the whole time from the highest window of the ashen house.

A pearly sky on the brink of snow moved into place over the syncline of mountains, and the breeze strengthened, whipping over the stone wall. Lungeing on towards the summit, the son kept looking back down at his home, surprised that with each of his small steps it shrank into the distance. Though he was breathless, his steps lightened as he walked further away from home. The summit offered him the glory of a perch from which to see the huge world beyond. His frail home appeared more brittle than an heirloom broken by every familial hand it had passed through. He looked strong.

We sat together on the same cold rock facing west, catching our breath back from the air that took it from us in that brisk exchange. A light pierced the sky and the far moor glowed umber. Cloud shadows slid in feral procession over the mountains and settled on the moor, which darkened to a plain of tenebrous copper until the shadows were pulled towards us by the breeze, and the moor regained its various glows of blond mahogany. The ray of light widened over the land, parting the snow-stuffed clouds, baring a blue sky as frail as a snowflake.

The son was in silence during the whole show of colour. His breathing was quieter than the breeze, though he shivered in his young bones, so we made our way down through small lanes of rock and mud, down the least-trodden way of Raven Mountain, towards the stream that sparkled through a plain of black-ink bog, and ran down to the edge of his father's field. The father was waiting for him by the sheep pen to mend the wire that bound the keep of corrugated tin walls. There was whisky on his breath. He squinted in the bright winter noon, nodded to me as I walked home, then passed his son pliers, a hammer, and a handful of new staples.

Time Alone Heals

From the top of Lucky Tor I stood halfway between the night sky of golden stars and the night ground of silver frost. Windless and still, the air carried every sound to its clearest pitch and every colour to its clearest hue. I had never before needed to squint to look at the full moon. It shone like a white sun without heat.

Down from the heights of the tor a fire, no bigger than a star above, standing out amidst the world of white and black frost, crackled and wavered. Smoke flurried up in slow plumes, gusting in strobes across the moon that burned through like a ghostly corona, then vanished into the night. My breath raced after the rising fumes but fell out of sight less than a metre from my eyes. The fire and the river were loud, the mingling roar interrupted now and again by the call of a screech owl that seemed to yell from only a tree away. In the fire's warmth a dark figure sat, a shadow: my brother, hunched as close as possible to the heat without getting burned, as far as possible from the tide of ice that closed in around him. I couldn't take my eyes away from the image of the fire, the hunched shadow with a whisky bottle in his lap, and the River Dart sweeping down through black rocks tumbling in white and silver silks.

I shuffled down from the tor, clambering over boulders and thick pillows of moss, breaking sticks as I trod, and took my place beside my brother. He smiled at me, then we blew into the fire, shoulder to shoulder, reviving the embers that were close to dying out, killing off the freeze that was close to claiming us. The frost glittered gold in the reflected light of the fire, and the whisky shone silver with the light of the moon.

Driving towards Dartmoor, I tried to think of when my brother and I had last spent time together like this. There were childhood memories, of course: running from waves on the beach by home, building rickety camps in the back-garden hedges, lobbing mud grenades at fences, catapulting apples onto the neighbour's roof, and leaping from the crumbling cliffs into the soft slides of sand below. But between then and now seemed to be wide gaps of time where memories should be. Only snippets of contact, short visits, going our separate ways as siblings so often do, wrapped up in settling down our own roots elsewhere. For the past five years he had been in Arkansas, where I had paid only a week's visit. Before his leaving for America, except for childhood antics I really could not recall a wholesome time together.

When by late afternoon we reached the point where the West Dart River runs into the East Dart, the bright winter sun had receded from the valley, leaving a light that was not yet dusk but was not part of day; a limbo of colour. Bare oaks were struggling to show themselves in the darkening air above the darker rivers that blended into one long rush of sound, pouring into one another beneath the stone arch of the clapper bridge. Light and warmth were leaving the valley, and darkness and cold were taking over. Our breath haloed the first stars as together we stared up at the night sky from the road. Leaving the car behind, we took the first steps of the path that hugged the bank of the river, then, after half an hour of walking in the dark, veered up left through a small wood that took us above the treeline. My collies, Daisy and Dilly, dashed ahead, prancing up and then down the long and steep slope of heather that stayed on our left as we descended a series of close steps into a pitch-black wood. My head torch flickered on, illuminating the white-foil strips of a lone silver birch's bark. The eyes of my dogs bobbed like two hares, then vanished, followed by rustling in the undergrowth, then the shining eyes would return, four of them, bright and curious, watching our awkward walk over and around boulders that were growing skins of ice as we walked further into the night.

I listened to my brother's heavy footsteps, not mine, clomp on the boulder path. I heard, too, his rough hands, calloused by years of hard work, make contact with the rough pelt of a rock or a tree as he leaned down for support. I listened to his breathing, which rose and fell, rose and fell, quicken when the path snaked up and slow when the path descended to the bank of the river. I listened to my brother's movements so closely as I walked that I soon lost sight and hearing of my own.

We stopped together to gaze into the river that seemed miles off by sight but inches close by sound, but even in those few moments of rest the strengthening cold got too much to bear so we kept on walking, looking into the water that slid and tumbled onwards as we walked, casting no reflections, tumbling without mirrors.

Pure and dark like the blood of night, the river beat its drum, clashed its cymbals, making a song that was our anthem as we trudged for hours in the dark, then fading out as we came into the Dart-side clearing. Here was to be our camp for the next two nights. My brother went to gather firewood, the dogs followed, and I pitched the tent at the clearing's far end.

Fullest of moons, bare black oak blooming with the moon's glow. Facing the tent porch towards Lucky Tor, I ditched our luggage inside and laid out our sleeping bags side by side. It took a while to get the fire going, every stick and snap of kindling was damp and cold, making the fire smoke heavy enough to veil the tor and our eyes from one another. Once the heat of the fire was established, the smoke gave way to a clear, bright flame we fed with choice branches that were drying in stacks at the fire's edge. I couldn't take my eyes off the fire's shadow projected hugely onto the granite wall.

We said little; there was enough to listen to. Even the three-storey-high bulk of granite seemed to express a sound that was audible only if we listened the most we had ever listened before. The cold pushed us closer to the warmth of the fire; it brought us shoulder to shoulder.

Firelight rode up my brother's boots, jeans, sleeves, and jacket. Moonlight and firelight mingled in the glassy arenas of his wide eyes. Wrinkles stretching from the outside tips of his eyes to his ears were as dark and as deep as the cut lines in the granite he faced. Etched by weather, the pain of hard worry, graced by a smile as he looked towards me through thin moonlit smoke, it was as though I saw my brother's face for the first time. After stuffing more half-dried branches into the fire, we walked briskly over to the big river to wash our pots and pans. I knelt into the cold hard ground, feeling the chill air slide down the back of my neck, and filled my pots and pans with moonlit water. My brother left me to clean his pans as he skipped over boulders submerged in shadow and stood at the edge of a shelf of black rock. Below, a deep torrent of sparkling moonlight burst through a gap between two rocks and sped away into the darkness beyond. Above the roar I couldn't hear him as he called out to me; only a small shadow with a mouth moved.

Our first night's sleep was restless at best. The fire spluttered and fizzled out by midnight, the ash froze, wore a mantle of frost. The dogs, cramped between us in the sagging tent, gave out a homely warmth. I listened to the river most of the night, my brother's cold breathing, and thought of the granite outside our door keeping guard over two brothers.

Dawn light had yet to fill the valley. The air was painfully cold as I shivered forward to yank open the tent flap with a flimsy zip. My brother rose, rubbing his eyes, yawning. He looked tired. I'm sure I did too. Pulling on jumpers, hats, and jackets, we crawled out into the waning dusk of a predawn dark, grey like stone. Scuffing the ash, breaking the mould of ice, my brother kneeled to ignite a firelighter pursed carefully between his hands. The dogs followed me into the birch and oak wood via the river, in which I washed the sleep from my face.

Back at the tent, a small flame flickered over wood, budding into enough of a fire with the sticks I had gathered to warm our bodies and breakfast. Over beans, toast, and coffee, the blue sky began to emerge and the valley steamed, the ice loosening its grip. The plan, devised in chattering monosyllables over breakfast, was to simply seek out warmth, to find the sun. That meant climbing back out of the pit of the Dart Valley, onto the moors and into the never-ending blue of the sky.

We took what we needed for the day and walked on past the granite wall that seemed to watch us as we moved, irking its presence. When I leaned on my brother's strong arm to help me over a rock I leaned upon a limb of Dartmoor, and when I looked into his deep hazel eyes I looked into an old wood haunted by the ghosts of nature's bygone worshippers. When we talked as we ascended the steep moorside stubbled with heather, I talked to the voice of the River Dart and the crisp, clean air of the moor.

Following the river too far into an impasse of fallen boulders, hemmed in by thicket and low branches, we turned off, and slowly climbed the hillside through frosted bracken that crunched like hollow bones beneath our boots. Climbing steadily, we soon got warm.

On flatter ground, at the top of the moor's shoulder, a cold, fast wind blew across, combing down the golden grasses, whistling off rock lumps scattered here and there. The wind grew colder and stronger and, by noon, was belting across the moor, forcing us to take shelter behind a tor that, according to the map, had no name. Clouds grouped on the horizon, and with the force of the wind were soon making their way, a vast sheet of grey darkly bruised and heavy with rain, maybe sleet, maybe snow, over the moor and the sky. The sun gone, buried in dark cloud, and a biting wind that wouldn't let up, made for a cold day, squeezing out any residue of the warmth we'd managed to glean from the morning's walk. Thick sleet shot diagonally across the wide, stormy moor that seemed to rock to and fro like a lost sea. Snow, too, carpeted the heather and then, by mid-afternoon, heavy and cold rain poured down.

Heads bowed, backs bent, we leaned forward into the skin-killing wind, cutting off through an escarpment that led us to a swollen river flayed by rain that gushed and lashed down from growing clouds. We sat close together, my brother and I. All we could do was laugh and shiver through our laughter, cupping our steaming coffees with both hands as we hunkered down in the shocks of rain that hissed electric across rocks and grass. The dogs were quite comfortable, although I could spy a glimmer of boredom in their restless eyes. Altering our plan to cross the full length of the moor, we trudged down sodden, shin-deep heather, following a small river that cut its way, banked by crumbling barrels of leaking soil and peat, to the River Dart. Dusk was soon upon the land, hauling the night in its wake. The rain did not cease, but nor did our happiness. Crossing back over the river along sunken stepping stones wasn't an option, so we had to retrace our path back up out of the valley, across the moor by night, re-entering the valley on the correct side of the river, where, mercifully, our tent was waiting.

Rain whipped the tor and poured down its face in ribbons that, given the night, would freeze into pools at the granite's base. A bird, raven or owl, flicked sluggishly off a crooked branch overhanging the tent, lifting slowly up through the pummelling weight of the rain. The dogs chased after it, skidding to an abrupt halt at the river's edge, barking into the darkness that couldn't muster an echo.

Miraculously my brother got a fire going; it fizzed in the rain. Our wet clothes steamed by the fire, our boots boiled. The dogs took shelter in the tent, nuzzling deep into our sleeping bags. We remained outside through the worst of the cold rain, cooking supper, sipping coffee. After a bleary two hours the rain subsided to a dense drizzle and then ceased, leaving behind a wrecked world and a loud, loud river that drowned out the sounds of the fire and our speech. By midnight the clouds had cleared and the sodden land around us began to freeze. I could have stayed awake all night breathing in the winter scent of things, the fire's aroma, the fragrant trees budding with stars, the tor's coolness. The land took on a vivid freshness.

Even though the river thundered and the streams pattered down through the wood like falling crowds of men, there was a definite quiet in that place. The longer we patiently stoked the fire and shared in each other's stillness, the more a silence took shape in the things around us, and within us. My brother felt it too, I could see it in his eyes and the way he sat up straight from slouching into a poise of vigilance. The dogs, too, shook sleep from their fur and stepped out from the tent to bask in the silence. It shone through every bare branch, every part of the tingling, chill air.

It was as though my brother and I had crossed a barrier and stepped forth into a new world that was yet strangely familiar, before the need to name. We rose from the logs around the fire and were irresistibly drawn to the maze of rocks around the foot of the tor. Playing amongst them, climbing over them higher and higher as though recovering a secret staircase from the ruined house of the world, we clambered onto the top of Lucky Tor and gazed out over the moonlit ocean of the moor. Like a ship being taken deeper and further out from what we have known, the tor seemed to drift and whirl, dip and rise.

Up on the high granite platform, my brother and I blew the sparks of the stars into a flame that warmed us. We were let into the land, together. Separate constellations togged together and became a single luminous round hollow in the night sky, its edges lit by the moon, drawing out the air in our lungs to the very last breath, making us utterly empty and weightless, lifting us and lighting us over the Dart Valley. Moors rolled and reeled backwards beneath us as we soared along a route of white-gold light that shone out from the earth.

I awoke the next morning to the rain hitting the tent side and the dogs stretching over me, eager to be let out. Was it a dream, that vision? All of it – the clear moonlit night, my brother and me being held aloft by an earth-light towards the truest of all homes beaming in the night sky – was it a dream? I turned to my brother, who was snoring, his sleeping face hidden in a mess of hood, jumper, and jacket. After an hour or so he came to and we sidled out of the tent, shivering in the cold rain that seemed to leak into our bones. Deciding to walk out of the valley and head home, we packed away all our things, brought down the tent and tidied up the remains of the fire. I took one last look at the granite face of the tor as we followed the curve of the wood upriver and walked steadily for hours through grey rain that stuck to us like fine filaments.

The dogs showed contentment in their eyes as they snuggled down in dry blue blankets in the back of the car and switched off to sleep for the long drive home. As we left Dartmoor behind, following the narrow, dipping lanes out into the known world, tors rose up from the dim surroundings like luminous mini mountains. My brother was knocked out by sleep, his head thrown back against the headrest, his mouth open, his Adam's apple protruding. I drove on in silence, cold and happy.

Mary

Now you are not here I think of one leaf
safe from snow beneath a resting fox's tail.
When he runs I will rush to bring to mind
all the warm light I know:

Your grey eyes
like ovals of tracing paper eclipsing the sun.
Your hands, like Mum's, wrinkled and larger,
lined with ashes of care,

knitting the colours of time
into a garment that will never fray
through the endless frost of your absence.

Grandma Mary

Grandma Mary's last words to me, as I cautiously step through her white bedroom door, Dad inches behind in his all-white tennis gear, his big Asics trainers clipping my heel, are: 'Oh, William, your acne looks so much better.'

After her strained whisper, the softness of her West Yorkshire tone like a cushion under the words, I stop halfway between the door and the bed, and dab my face with each of my fingers.

Mum is sitting on a low stool as close as she can get to the bedside, slightly hunched over in a languid arc, her knees lodged into the mattress side. They share a single woollen blanket, mother and daughter, most of it draped over Grandma. Mum's hands are neatly folded into a small ball like a wren's nest in the dip of the blanket between her thighs. Mum looks tired but not as tired as Grandma. Mum is glad to see me, to see Dad. Grandma doesn't smile but I can tell, in a familiar look she gives, that she is glad to have her family around her during the last afternoon of her life. One white pillow is placed beneath each arm. Three pillows, each garlanded with white hems of lace, prop up her neck and head. But she looks low down, far away.

Along my jawline, up my cheeks, around my nose and chin, are raised patches of sore Braille, tender and lumpy. My fingertips tremble over my bobbled face as though I'm overtaken by a nervous disbelief. I turn from Grandma, though her eyes are wearily fixed upon me as though waiting for a reply, her head slightly tilted to one side, her pale expression bereaved of living warmth, her skin like a bouquet of fading lilies. I pass around Dad, through his robust smell of sweat shed after our three sets of tennis at Bournemouth Gardens (a ploy agreed between him and Mum to limit my time with the dying), I cross the dim hallway, enter the cramped bathroom, then abruptly put my face up to the small square mirror. A glass bowl is half filled with potpourri on a shelf below, with an unlit tea light either side of it, two wicks curled over at the tip like black grass stems. Who will light them?

Grandma must have been lying or was under an illusion, because my face is beaming with raised dots that, as I peer in closer, nose to nose with myself, resemble chains, circles, geographies of weeping volcanoes. Switching on the strip light above the mirror, I poke around in my face with eyes and fingers in a forensic rage of inspection; a unique detective work practised over years. My acne has been worsening despite my mum's and Grandma Mary's gentle tactics to make me feel better about how embarrassingly stupid I look. The spots that are acutely painful are usually the ones hidden beneath my eyebrows or clinging like tender barnacles to the inside of my nose. I flinch when I touch these, or catch them with my nail during a thoughtless scratch. 'It's bad luck to have long nails,' Grandma would say in the past, 'especially on Sundays.' One of her many superstitions.

I am always taken back by how red a face can really get. Sometimes it makes me laugh like a clown, those extreme scales of redness. At other times, particularly before school, I often attempt to puncture my skin with pins and scissors, hoping to relieve the pressure. Sometimes it looks as though I have been slapped all night, my skin tender and raw. Mutant mornings, I call them. From lathering toothpaste on my face to applying bio yoghurt, or simply rubbing my face senseless with a loofah, I have tried and tested most remedies. The only one that has any visible effect is sunlight, summer sunlight, wind, and sea. Every waking moment outside.

This November Sunday, on Sunny Moor Road, at Grandma's bungalow, face to face with my teenage grotesqueness, is surely one of the worst cases of acne I have ever seen. I should take a photograph, press tissues against my face and preserve the grease, take specimens. Quite disgusted, holding either side of the green ceramic basin, I slowly draw my head back and look past my face in the mirror into the bedroom behind me, at Mum kneeling down at Grandma's side. The bedroom is dark, as though it is already dusk, the dread of Monday school readying itself to pounce, but the bathroom clock says three. I watch in the mirror a little longer: Mum coming down off the stool and kneeling, pushing the top of her head into the neck of her mum, nuzzling. Grandma weakly lifts her left hand and lets it rest upon her daughter's back, rising and falling as Mum tries to breathe through her tears. Grandma's limbs are so weightless that the pillows beneath her are plump. She looks so light that even the shadows could take her, or she could be whisked away as a twirl of dust in the turn of a chill draught. We are all waiting.

Having never heard Mum cry before, it makes me awkward, vulnerable. Dad edges further into the dark room from the doorway, kneels down beside Mum, and rests his head on her shoulder. I wonder if Mum can smell Dad's body odour, if she even cares. Grandma tries to raise herself up and shift over to hold Mum more but is too weak and falls back again, the cancer pinning her down from within, detonating every second. She winces as though trying to figure out an answer to a really hard question, knowing time is running out to find it. I wish there were someone to turn the hourglass.

I feel as though I shouldn't be witnessing what is happening. I yank the frayed cord of the light switch, and the bathroom goes dark in a clunk. The cord swings and taps the mirror nine times before it comes to a standstill. I wash my hands with chalky soap in the dark, run water that I cannot see. I stand motionless in the hallway that is only shades lighter than the bedroom, not knowing where to go. Crossroads.

Mum is still holding on desperately to Grandma. Dad is now sitting on a straight-backed chair beside them both, beneath Grandma's huge pyramid of teddy bears piled up high. Maybe three more bears and the ceiling would be touched by a brown and cheerful head. But there won't be time for us to buy Grandma any more bears. It is Sunday, too, stores are all closed. Hundreds of black eyes stare down upon my family, smiling. Some bears are in Christmas jumpers, some in skirts or frocks, some in dungarees holding crimson hearts out in front of them like offerings or shields, some holding ornaments or with fat arms held up in Vs above their heads in surrender, or cheering. And the whole pyramid is shot through, splashed, with a rainbow of colours. Whoever has the bears after Grandma will need room enough in their home.

Turning away from the bedroom, I walk only a few steps through deep, plush carpet that parts and spreads through my toes like pelt, and come into the dining-room part of the kitchen. It is lighter in here, filled with a different kind of silence; a silence pleated into knots that dangle like grips from object to object, safer than the sinkhole of silence widening and deepening in the bedroom.

My bare feet slap on the cold black and white tiles of the floor. I remember counting the number of tiles once when Grandma was looking after me and I was bored and eating biscuit after biscuit, opening and closing every drawer, ransacking the place for some treasure, for some rare thing that might unlock a new world and explain everything. And Grandma seemed the type of person that would have the most special things on earth.

Attached to the counter that half divides the dining room and kitchen, fixed to the wall, a glass cabinet with sliding doors contains porcelain figurines, mostly foxes. Standing either side of the foxes is the Russian doll that I would, years ago, pull apart and abandon in dire dismemberment on the counter, the smallest one rolling from side to side, clutching a sprig of wheat in its arms, its rosy infant face painted with a look of bewilderment, a dot of blue on each cheek to resemble dimples, or spots. Grandma would slot and twist them back together with her right hand whilst her left hand was busy holding a cigarette, the smoke drifting up, crawling across the ceiling like a giant spider of murky vapour, the Silk Cut packet and lighter side by side on the counter in front of her like faithful attendants to her routine summons.

Even when we played with the porcelain foxes, their burnished coats, slick crimson and orange, bright in the sun that came in through the bay window, Grandma was mostly silent. I loved this silence. Through it, I always felt she was really with me. It was not the silence of wandering elsewhere in her head, but of being fully with me and being nowhere else. Her silence made the foxes matter in our games, made them the most important thing that day. Her hand, colder than the porcelain, held the foxes as though they were the most precious gifts in the world; not precious like expensive jewels, forbidden to the clumsy disregard of children, but precious because I had touched them, precious because I gave them life, put heart through my fingertips into their hollow bodies, and set them running across the counter, along the floor, leaping, lying down to rest with the cub in the nook of Grandma's tartan scarf lying in a bunch on the kitchen counter.

Standing in the middle of the kitchen, I stare now at the foxes behind the museum glass of the cabinet as though they are out of reach, preserved in some irredeemable channel of time. The Russian doll gazes back at me, a figure of indifference. Mum is no longer crying. Everything is a shadow of itself. The clock is loud. I can hear the baritone hum of Dad's voice but not the words. Death is such a big event. And Grandma isn't one for the limelight.

By three thirty, the dense layer of taupe clouds have been shifted south by the nudging edge of a northerly wind, revealing a blue sky that lacks radiance, a perfunctory substitute for the overcast day. I walk over to the stainless-steel sink and look out through the window. The blue washing line, stretched from one side of the garden to the other, strung with wooden pegs, sways in the wind like the string tapered between two plastic cups held to the ears of two friends. I can see Grandma out there – as I stood there once or twice – reaching up to grab the line whilst at the same time trying to smoke, pulling the line down to eye level and nonchalantly selecting a wooden peg from the floral cloth bag that I held, in her care while Mum was away at work. Her hand would clatter in the bag of pegs, and she would pull one out like a humble prize from a lucky dip that she was chuffed to win. Her dark red hair autumnal, her quiet presence like a hearth I was drawn to, her few words like leaves drifting, drifting about my eyes through the summer sky of her silence – I was going to miss that. And the pieces of clothing drafted along the line like a set of blessings to brighten and come to life in the sun. Fifteen pegs, I count, are left on the line.

Once when she was washing dishes she was struck by lightning, but her yellow Marigolds saved her. So Mum said. Standing by the stainless-steel sink, spotless and shining in the glow of the winter light, I can hardly imagine what it would have been like ... how shocked and frightened she must have been. Or not. Because her bravery through her life is incredible. A heart condition from birth, a domineering mother with a violent Catholicism, ousted to a convent, a husband with manic depression who, therefore, could not work, very little income, ice on the inside of the windows through Mum's formative years, a husband afflicted by Parkinson's and Alzheimer's, and lung cancer, at first misdiagnosed as a broken rib before she was told she had six months to live, but most likely less. She had been tried and yet never wanted for more than her family to be near. The simplicity of her needs is inspiring.

I think about Grandma's life as I stand gazing out of the window onto the bare winter garden, holding the taps that she held when she got struck by lightning. About it all, though, she is silent and through her silence her family draws near to her. She is never bitter about what she has been put through, never. She is a person of noble acceptance, of an uncontrived gratitude for everything. I know, too, that she is a good and warm person because Ollie, my Border terrier and closest friend, never leaves her side. Ollie would press his body against her leg as she sat deep in the armchair at Mum and Dad's, always watching and listening, never intruding, quietly delighting in her family being near.

At the far end of the kitchen, I look over the medicines stacked in rows along pinewood shelving. Between the medicine bottles and leaflets stand photographs in old silver frames. Me and my brother, shoulder to shoulder, brandishing red and blue spades at Sandbanks beach, Grandma throwing her head back in laughter on a deckchair in the sun, wearing opaque amber-brown sunglasses, the same blanket over her knees that is over her thin body in the cold bedroom, over her bruised and crumpled skin. Photographs of family, her life's work, her estate. I feel as though she comes from a place in which we all love one another and are not alone, and are warm, and enough for one another.

Will she take the love away with her when she goes? Or will the love she has for us remain, entrusted to us? What will life and death allow? What goes on between them, life and death, those occupants of the same house, talking about their work around a circle of embers, each ember a life glowing and fading under their instruction?

Past the pine cupboards, I step back into the dark hallway, and into Grandma's bedroom. Nothing has changed but something has changed. The indoor air, the mood, the light and shadow, the silence, the presence of an extensive edge over which the world teeters. A breath of life has left and we all feel the blow so acutely we feel sick with it. Mum incredibly so, bunched up in pain, lying beside her mum on the bed. A silence takes over the room and strikes us dumb, a sheet of ice in a frozen darkness sliding over us. We claw our way towards her even though she has drifted, is not drifting, away. She is already in the past, and her body asks for us, asks for her daughter to witness its fading. There is no preparation that could have tempered this rupture, and in this respect is renewed. I have completely forgotten about my acne.

Sidestepping the foot of the bed, I stand on the opposite side to Mum and Dad. The window is open. A breeze blows through, lifting a white curtain sash into the air like a flag of surrender. Through the window, I look out onto a deep blue sky fluttering with the first kindling of sunset. A blackbird, with a holly berry in its bill, shoots past the window and dives into the neighbour's hedge. A single car trundles by. I lock eyes with the driver in slow motion, his face almost featureless behind the dark glass of the car window. I watch the white-linen sash move elegantly in the air, casting a play of very faint shadows over the white bed, over Grandma, who is stiller than I could ever have imagined. Mum is curled up beside her like a child. Dad is sitting, his head bowed, hands folded, on the chair beneath the cliff of teddy bears. It is so quiet, absolute. Not like a beginning or an end, but something else. A span of space before change, the space from which change happens.

I kneel at the bedside, and look at Grandma. Where did she go? She looks like she might wake up at any moment. The world tilts, the loss of her more immediate to me than my own self, my own skin. But I don't understand. She is there, right there, in front of me, in the centre of the bed. She is not there, though.

As our car leaves her home around midnight – after the rest of the family have been, the coroner, other visitors too late to say their prayers – I swiftly look back through the rear window and see Grandma standing beneath the street light, cast in an orange glow, waving goodbye, waving in the way she did that was a celebration, a welcome, a calling. Her arm would swing from side to side in the air like a stuck clock hand marking a point in time in which things neither come nor go, but stay. And I could feel her waving even as I turned the corner, and was miles off down the road, in the forest, near the sea, back home, through the door, to the happy barking of Ollie and the ignored schoolwork lying open on the kitchen table.

During the funeral, as the coffin is sprayed with earth by hands old and young, I spot through the dark crowd of mourners a fox looking right at us, at me. I tug on Mum's sleeves, and Dad's. They look up, and see the fox staring at us from behind the headstones until, breaking the gaze, it bolts into the hedge.

Afterword

Elowen

Reading of parenthood
from the growth rings of an oak tree
rippling out
through ageing infancy
from the heartwood,

the image comes to mind,
Elowen,
of many concentric circles
spreading
from the tips of your fingers
when you first touch
a body of water.

Two years ago today a swallow flew into our house through the back door and landed on the white window sill. Sunlight streamed in through the windows, highlighting a beam of dust that floated around her like a veil. Her long wings lay out either side of her blue-black body. She twitched her head from side to side. I approached her, thinking she would pelt off and flutter all over the room before she found her way out, but she stayed. Possibly terrified, exhausted. The first swallow of the year, thousands of miles weary. Her dark eyes glinted. Sliding my right hand beneath her, her feet gently yielding to the movement of my hand, I carried her quickly outside, lifted my arm up and down to encourage her take-off. But she stayed put, seemingly relaxed. She looked about at the surroundings, tipping her head to the green ground and the blue sky.

I sat down on the bench with the swallow upon my hand. She stepped out of my palm and shuffled to the end of my outstretched forefinger. She even preened herself, jittering her biro-tip beak into her flank, parting the tiny feathers. I attempted again to give her purchase, moving my arm up and down out in front of me. She stayed still. I brought her back in close, closer to my eye. I touched the forefinger of my left hand against her chest, hoping to feel the drum of her minute heart. With a rustle of wings and rearranging of feet, she stirred up and dived into the air, flying in a straight line two feet from the ground, then, in a quick arc, she double-backed, chattering, and clipped over my head, following the ridge line of the roof, out of sight.

Today two swallows have made their nest beneath the roof of the dilapidated hut at the back of our garden beside the yew tree. The fuzzy heads of nestlings peer up now and again over the edge of the nest. I look in from afar.

Two weeks from today is the due date of our daughter, Elowen. Last summer, we lost our first after five weeks of pregnancy. We wrote *Seed* into the grey sand of a beach in the far north-west corner of Washington State, that epithet washed away by the Pacific. Back home, Amy and I went into hiding for two weeks, finding solace in simple chores, walking in the woods with Daisy and Dilly.

Now we are in a state of waiting and preparing the home for Elowen's arrival. Like the nestling swallows – their downy fluff sprouting the first feather, their flight muscles budding cell by cell, their being aligning to the great rhythms of migration that will soon envelop them – her body, too, is building for the seasons, her lungs maturing, the lanugo almost gone. Her eyes, opening and closing, see the changes in light made by the trees upon her mother's skin, her ears hear our voices, even perhaps the swallows nattering first thing outside our open bedroom window.

At night I rest my hands upon Amy's belly, waiting for the movements, the kicks, the high fives, the pressing loll of Elowen's body as she shifts position, getting herself ready. In the quiet I hear the nightjar, out on the heath, drilling its rapid anthem of mystery into the wall of stars. The nestling swallows are sleeping now, as are the parents. Elowen sleeps. I lift my hand from Amy's belly, and turn onto my left side. And so the threads of life continue, the broken pieces are mended once more.

Acknowledgements

I would firstly like to thank my wife, Amy, for always believing in me whenever I wanted to give up, and for her unending love and support. She is an inspiration.

My daughter, Elowen, who passed away during the book's development. I do everything for her, to make her proud. She is the beautiful ring of light that surrounds all that I behold.

And my family for reading and rereading everything I've ever written, and believing in me too.

Thank you to my agent for believing in me and putting my book forward to the most amazing and supportive team at Penguin Random House.

To my editor, Joanna Taylor, for bringing out the essence of the book and giving me so much confidence in my work.

And last but not least my two furry hounds, Daisy and Dilly, for always taking me further into the woods and over more mountains.